SPIRITUAL COMBAT

in the

INVISIBLE WAR

*Dark Angels Encounter the
People of Light*

WILLIAM L. PROBASCO

Archway Publishing books may be ordered through booksellers or by contacting:

Archway Publishing
1663 Liberty Drive
Bloomington, IN 47403
www.archwaypublishing.com
844-669-3957

Scripture taken from the New King James Version® Copyright © 1982 by Thomas Nelson. Used by permission. All rights reserved.

ISBN: 978-1-6657-0536-3 (sc)
ISBN: 978-1-6657-0537-0 (e)

Library of Congress Control Number: 2021907215

Print information available on the last page.

Archway Publishing rev. date: 05/27/2021

WHY A BOOK ABOUT ANGELS? PERSONAL ENCOUNTERS

I have believed in angels for as long as I can remember. I believe the Bible, and to read it is to learn that millions of angels are active in the universe. The subject was interesting but not necessarily important to me until I began to serve as a pastor. That is when I began encountering angels. Some of them were God's angels; others were dark angels—angels who serve Satan, called "demons."

God's Angels

I encountered some of the angels of God indirectly at first, through the testimony of a godly man. I have related that experience in chapter 1. Later, I beheld the splendor of one of the Lord's mighty angels early one morning in 1975.

I was given the opportunity to travel to England to attend the centennial meeting of an abundant life ministry in the Lake District, in the town of Keswick. Dr. Stephen Olford and Dr. Billy Graham were to be the keynote speakers in the two-week-long celebration. I had prayed and asked the Lord to make a way for me to go. Not long afterward, Dr. Olford asked me to lead a group of people who also wanted to attend "Keswick," and that is the way my prayer was answered.

As my departure date neared, my fear of flying began to haunt my thoughts. Early on the morning of departure, as I prepared to go to the airport, I gathered my family around me in the den and read Psalm 91:9–16, and then we prayed. I was to be gone three weeks. My kids were crying; I was stricken with fear. What if something happened to them or to me while I was gone? I asked God to give His angels charge over them and me. I also asked Him for a sign that He would provide for the protection of my family and me during the trip. I desperately needed reassurance.

I took my suitcase outside. I could see the headlights of a car off in the distance, probably my friend who would drive me to the airport. As I turned back to my left to say a final goodbye, a large angel appeared over my house and family, flying horizontally, face down with arms and hands extended and huge wings. He looked at me, smiling. He was bright and resplendent against the dark sky at four in the morning. He exuded strength and power. My fears melted away as I realized that God had answered my request for a sign. I turned away but then looked back, thinking it might be a hallucination. He was still there. A sound reverberated from him, one I had never heard.

That encounter was the only time I have ever had an angel reveal his presence to me. Although the experience was thrilling, I have not asked God for a repeat performance. I never try to pray to angels. That would be idolatry. They are with me to assist me as I obey the will of God in life and ministry. I am grateful to Him for allowing me to see one of His strong angels that morning. I felt the way Elisha's servant must have felt when God showed him a multitude of angels protecting them from the Syrian army. (2 Kings 6:17).

Satan's Angels

I was counseling a college girl one day, who said that she was being visited as she slept by "a being of some kind" who would appear like a dark shadow over her. It would choke her and threaten her in a strange voice. I began to search for the source of the "being" by asking her questions about her social life, dating, drugs, her worldview, possible occult involvement, and whether or not she had a relationship with Christ. During the interview I was shocked by a low-pitched, growling voice telling me to shut up and leave the girl alone. She became frightened and wanted to end the session. A dark angel—a demon—was obviously present in her body.

I had never met a demon before that incident. I did not know how to respond. The voice came out of her, but it was not her voice. It was another personality. When I asked for its name, the voice said, "Artesia." I stumbled through the confrontation by asking more questions. I finally told her that an unclean spirit had entered her sometime in the past. Finally, in the name of Jesus, I commanded the demon to come out of her.

How God's Angels Help Us

I did not realize then what I have since come to know, that God's angels play an essential role in meeting the spiritual needs of His people and His world. I was a student of the Bible, yet the vast amount of information it contains about good and evil angels had escaped me. Most Christians today are like I was then, having little or no biblical knowledge about angels, even though the Bible has more than three hundred references to the angels of God and about two hundred to demons and Satan.

Biblical knowledge about these invisible spiritual beings is not important just for the sake of knowledge. Every day, they are involved in our lives and in the progress of the Christian faith across the world. The angels of the Lord are ministering servants to us (Hebrews 1:14), while Satan's dark angels plan and execute strategies against us (Ephesians 6:12).

The apostle Paul exhorted us to cast off our lethargy and get serious about our invisible war with the devil and his angels:

> And do this, knowing the time, that now it is high time
> to awake out of sleep; for now our salvation is nearer

than when we first believed. The night is far spent, the day is at hand. Therefore let us cast off the works of darkness, and let us put on the armor of light. (Romans 13:11–12)

Beginning with chapter 1, we will examine the essential facts of angelology, the study of angels, good and evil. We will learn the answers to serious questions, such as "How and why do angels exist?" I am often asked, "Why are there evil angels? How are angels involved in human lives? Where did evil come from? How and why does Satan exist?" Of great importance is the Bible's explanation of the invisible war between good and evil angels and how we humans are part of that cosmic conflict. We will learn that behind evil humans are evil angels, promoting rebellion against God and determined to destroy Christians and take over the world. We will also learn about how dark angels, called "demons," can enter humans and occupy their spiritual nature, taking over their lives and using them to support Satan's master plan for world domination.

We will also learn how Jesus Christ, the Son of God, has defeated Satan and, through the law of the Spirit of life, can give freedom to anyone who has been made captive to Satan's power, in whatever form it may take. May you know the joy of abundant life in Jesus through victory in spiritual combat in the invisible war.

William Probasco

CONTENTS

ANGELS, GOOD AND EVIL

> For by Him all things were created that are in heaven and that are on earth, visible and invisible, whether thrones or dominions or principalities or powers. All things were created through Him and for Him. And He is before all things, and in Him all things consist. (Colossians 1:16–17)

Angels. Are they real? If so, what do they look like, and what is their purpose? How did they originate? The Bible says that there are both good angels and evil ones. A desperate war has been raging between them from before the creation of the world. Humans are involved, but most of us do not realize it because angels are invisible. Sometimes they appear, and we do not recognize them as angels because they are disguised as humans, usually as young men. The presence of evil angels (called dark angels and demons) can be known by the wickedness they promote, such as addictions, crimes, and sexual deviancy.

The Creation of the Angels

Angels Were Created by the Preexistent Son of God

The apostle Paul explained that the origin of angels was by the Son of God, who has always existed as God the Son. He was the creator of all angels. He created them when He was preexistent—before He came into the world and took on humanity. This is called the "incarnation," meaning God becoming man.

Before I continue, let me explain His incarnation. The Holy Spirit created His special human body in Mary. This miraculous conception enabled Him to retain His divine nature as God the Son and take the additional nature of humanity. He was God the Son as well as perfect man, existing in perfect harmony in one Person, Jesus the Christ. He was the perfect, personal, and permanent discloser of God to mankind. His deity and perfect humanity exist without conflict in the one Person, Jesus.

Now we go back to the creation of the angels. Long before Jesus was conceived in eternity past, He fulfilled the will of the Father by creating millions of angels. All were good angels at first.

Angels Were Created as Spiritual Beings

They have spirit bodies. The apostle Paul said that there are natural bodies and spiritual bodies (1 Corinthians 15:44). They can take material forms and appear as young men or any other appropriate form. As such, they can do things that humans do, such as walking, talking, and eating. They can do supernatural things in the material world, even though they are spiritual creatures. They are powerful. They can fly through space at the speed of light. Whenever it is necessary for them to fulfill a mission for God, they do it perfectly. A perfect example of an angelic mission is the following account out of my days as a young pastor.

Four Angels Visit a Hospital Room

During my seminary years I was the pastor of a village church in Texas. One day I received a frantic call from an elderly lady whose husband was experiencing severe chest pains. I jumped into my car and almost flew down the road to their farmhouse. I went inside and saw her husband, whom most of us called "Uncle Port," lying on a couch. His chest was heaving, and his face was turning dark. I scooped my arms underneath his small frame and carried him to my car. I slid him into the back seat, and then we sped the twelve miles to the nearest hospital. In the ER, competent medical personnel got him stabilized, and in a few hours, he was taken to a private room. Family and friends quickly gathered in the area. I worked my way to a corner of his bed, next to his head. He began talking to me even though he had been ordered by nurses to be quiet and rest.

Within another hour he seemed more like himself. He wanted to talk. "Pastor, do you remember preaching about angels and Elijah's chariot?"

I nodded. "Sure, Brother Port."

His next word was a shock to everyone, including me. "Well, four of them are here and have come to get me. They say I'm going with them."

I blurted out, "Do you really mean angels, Deacon?" He smiled and nodded to me. I thought he was hallucinating, but my old deacon began to point them out to me. There was one at each of the four corners of the bed, which meant that one was beside me.

I asked him what they looked like. "Like young men, maybe about your age, Pastor!"

His wife could stand no more talk about angels. She began to chide him, saying, "Oh, Papa, you're just seein' things."

He smiled and repeated what he had previously said about the four angels. Then he said, "No, Mama. I ain't seein' things. All of you listen! They are here with us. I'll be leavin' soon. I'm goin' with 'em!"

I still felt a bit skeptical, but I lost any doubt after that answer by Uncle Port to his wife. It was real, and my old farmer-deacon, a godly man, was telling us the truth about what he saw and heard. Four messengers from heaven had visited him and were at that moment quietly standing around his bed.

I bent down and kissed his forehead. Then I said, "Well, Deacon, I believe you. Now I guess I'd better get home. Whichever way this goes, I'll see you in the morning!"

"Yeah, Pastor, I'll see you in the mornin'." I knew he meant *resurrection* morning!

I played back the events of the day in my mind as I drove the twelve miles home. As I walked through the parsonage door, the phone was ringing. It was one of Uncle Port's family. "Pastor, Uncle Port just passed away." In my mind I replayed the scene in the hospital room. I imagined seeing the angels and Elijah's fiery chariot in the biblical passage Uncle Port referred to. I hummed the tune of the old spiritual: "A band of angels, a-comin' after me, comin' for to carry me home."

The mission of those four angels was to escort a Christian to his new home in heaven, prepared by Jesus for him (John 14:1–3).

Angels Are Not Humans Who Have Died

Angels were created to be angels, and humans were created to be humans. One does not become the other. Scripture never states or implies that humans who have died become angels.

A commonly held but false belief is that babies who die become angels. This is not scriptural, and therefore it is not true. A male child was conceived in the affair of King David with Bathsheba, the wife of one of his finest soldiers. The infant became mortally ill. David repented of his sin and asked the Lord to spare the child, but God took him to heaven. David explained:

> While the child was alive, I fasted and wept; for I said, "Who can tell whether the LORD will be gracious to me, that the child may live?" But now he is dead; why should I fast? Can I bring him back again? I shall go to him, but he shall not return to me. (2 Samuel 12:22–23)

So David would meet his little son in heaven. The child's spirit was taken to heaven. There is not so much as a hint that he would become an angel.

Angels Were Created to be God's Messengers and Servants

In both Testaments of the Bible we are told that God made His angels to be spirits. As His servants, they would reflect His glory, resembling a brilliant flame of fire (Psalm 104:4).

The word "angel" in the Hebrew Old Testament is *malakh,* meaning "messenger." In the Greek New Testament, the word for "angel" is *angellos,* also meaning "messenger."

Angels Are Given Supernatural Power

Angels can accomplish tasks that would be impossible for humans. Their physical strength, knowledge of coming events, warnings about impending disasters, and power to protect people are examples of the powers given to them.

Two angels appeared in the city of Sodom. They had been sent by God to destroy it. They looked like young men. Lot, nephew of Abraham, invited them to his home for a meal and lodging. Some of the men of Sodom became physically attracted to them and demanded that Lot send them outside for sexual purposes. Lot was shaken. He begged the men not to do such a wicked thing. He even offered them his daughters to fulfill their lust, but they refused. They only wanted to rape these handsome young men.

> But before they lay down, the men of the city, even the men of Sodom, both old and young, all the people from every quarter, surrounded the house. And they called to Lot and said to him, "Where are the men who came to you tonight? Bring them out to us that we may know them carnally." (Genesis 19:4–5)

The angels warned Lot that they had been sent to destroy the city because of the wickedness that permeated the lifestyles of most of the population. They ordered Lot to get his family and quickly leave Sodom:

> We will destroy this place, because the outcry against them has grown great before the face of the LORD, and the LORD has sent us to destroy it. (Genesis 19:13)

God gave the angels power to destroy an entire city, and four others. They had the awesome resources of strength, wisdom, and power, sending fire and sulfur raining down on the cities of Sodom, Gomorrah, Admah, Zeboiim, and Zoar (Genesis 14:8).

Angels Were Created Simultaneously and Permanently

There are no baby angels, though some artists insist on characterizing them as babies in everything from baby books to bathroom tissue. Angels were not born to angel parents. They were not "born" at all but were apparently created fully formed and will not be changed.

They are also sexless. Jesus said: "For in the resurrection they neither marry nor are given in marriage, but are like angels of God in heaven" (Matthew 22:30).

Angels Do Not Die

Angels do not cease to be. They never become extinct. The angels of God live in His presence forever. The fallen angels (demons) will one day be thrown into the lake of fire, but they do not die in the sense of becoming extinct. They will exist in a state of death forever. To exist apart from God is death.

The Angels of God Do Not Participate in New Age Fiction Such as Channeling

The claim of some New Age teachers that angels carry messages back and forth between us and our loved ones who have died is false. There is no hint of such a claim in the Bible. They are messengers, but there is no communication from us to spirits in eternity. In fact, Jesus said such a thing is impossible. When a beggar named Lazarus died, a wealthy man in hell asked Jesus to send him on a mission of mercy to dip his finger in water and cool his parched tongue. He also begged Jesus to send Lazarus to his family to warn them about hell.

Jesus replied to both requests to say that there is no way messages can be sent from here to eternity or from eternity to us: "And besides all this, between us and you there is a great gulf fixed, so that those who want to pass from here to you cannot, nor can those from there pass to us" (Luke 16:26).

Purveyors of occult magic often use angels as a way of substantiating their claims. Scripture has many passages that deal with evil angels and occult practices, but they show the reader how demons deceive people with false claims such as the claim of channeling.

Angels Were Created with Conscience and Freedom of Choice

When the archangel Lucifer instigated an attempt to overthrow God, he invited other angels to participate in his plan. About a third of them chose to act against God and help Lucifer invade heaven. This tragedy shows that angels have been given freedom of moral choice, just as humans. No act of angelic rebellion took place after this one.

Angels Are Spiritual Persons

Angels are not wisps of molecules or shadowy images, as seen on TV. They do not resemble clouds that move around the sky. They are not ghosts, apparitions, or hallucinations. They have spiritual bodies, not material ones as we have. Yet we contain a spiritual nature within our material bodies. We are designed to be "trichotomous," spirit, soul, and body. Because we have a sin nature, our spirits are dead toward God before we are saved. Jesus died and rose again so that the Holy Spirit can restore our spirits to life. This is called "regeneration."

Each angel is a unique personality, like humans but with greater capacity. They possess the three essential characteristics of personality: intellect, emotions, and will.

Angels are intellectual beings. They have intelligence unequalled by humans. In Scripture we see them rendering exalted worship of God (Psalm 148:2). They have great knowledge and wisdom, even knowing all things that are in the earth (2 Samuel 14:20). They sense danger and protect the people of God (Psalm 91:10–12).

They are emotional beings. If they were not, they could never give such intelligent and sincere worship to God as they do. They differ from humans in that they keep their emotions under perfect control. No selfish anger, pride, or other destructive feelings are observed in the angels of God. This is not true of the fallen angels, however, whose emotions were turned against the Lord through the influence of Lucifer. They hate God and all who worship and follow Him. They hate Jesus, the Son of God, with a contentious hostility that knows no bounds. In my counseling ministry I have often observed that when demons are confronted with the fact of the Lordship of Jesus Christ, many of them lose control and become belligerent and combative.

They are volitional beings. They possess a will. They worship and serve God because they desire to do so. They render enraptured praise and honor to Him. The fallen angels exercise their wills to obey Satan. About a third of the angels elected to follow him in his plot to overthrow God and all of creation. There is no way for them to reverse that decision. They will be incarcerated forever in the lake of fire at the judgment of the white throne (Revelation 20).

These characteristics were observable in a man who came to me for counseling and claimed that he could see what he called the "virgin aura" in women.

The Man Who Saw the "Virgin Aura"

In one of my pastorates, a group of four ministers asked me to meet a strange individual who had the reputation of being a wild man and dangerous to anyone who tried to change his way of life. Even police were afraid to take him into custody because a savage spirit of anger would come over him when they tried to apprehend him. At times he was known to destroy property and threaten to kill people. The ministers told me that he could bend a crowbar with his bare hands.

This man would sometimes enter a restaurant or other public gathering to look for women who had what he described as the "virgin aura." He said a light would appear over a woman's head when he entered the room. Only he could see it. The light was a signal to him that she wanted to "mate" with him. This claim led to some serious altercations. Men were badly hurt when they attempted to protect their wives or girlfriends from his brutal advances.

He lived in the woods in a makeshift cabin, living off the land and harassing people to give him food and money. Out of fear, they obliged him, although some wanted to shoot him.

As these ministers met to discuss how they might help him, the subject of demon possession came up because he closely resembled the Gadarene demoniac (see Mark 5:1ff and Luke 8:26ff), both in appearance and behavior. As they began looking for someone who might know how to deal with this type of problem, my name was mentioned. They phoned me to ask if they could bring him to see me, assuming he would accept their agreement to let them bring him. They promised to give him food and clothing that he needed.

When they arrived, I asked him general questions about his life. When I got around to the "virgin aura," he seemed excited about describing it to me. He thought he had power that no other men have, a magical power to attract a woman and cause her to desire him. He said that this power was from God.

When I told him that God would never do such a thing, his mood became defensive. I told him that this so-called power had been destructive, causing other people to fear him. I also told him that it was not God but an evil spirit that gave this so-called "virgin aura" to him. I suggested that if he would permit me to lead us all in prayer, we could ask Jesus to remove it from him, because He had been victorious over Satan in His death and resurrection.

The mention of the Lord's death and resurrection caused a red-hot wrath to break over the man's countenance. He left the chair and dropped to the floor of my office. He began crawling on all fours and growling, like a bear or wolf. I knew for sure he had one and probably more dark angels controlling him. Demons hate Jesus, His cross, His blood, His resurrection, and His Lordship with a hatred that one must see to believe. I had lit a fuse, and he was about to explode.

His eyes turned red. His body shook. The growling became intense and threatening.   He continued crawling toward me. My stomach knotted. I challenged him by saying, "You want to kill me, don't you?"

His reply was, "I'm *gonna* kill you, preacher!" The four ministers jumped up to restrain him. He shoved them away. He wanted to get his big hands on me. Though I was afraid of being badly hurt, I had to take things to the next level, the evil power in him versus the invincible power of the Holy Spirit. I commanded him, by the authority of the Lord Jesus Christ, to stop crawling and growling and to sit back down.

He glared at me for a few seconds and then dropped his head like a scolded puppy. He stood up, walked backward to the chair, and sat down. I was relieved. I then said, "You see? Inside you is an evil spirit, not God but an angel of the devil. He makes you mad at Jesus and at me. Let's kneel down by our chairs and pray and ask Jesus to take the evil spirit out of you."

He replied, "*No!* I *like* him in there! He makes me strong and important! People are afraid of me. Let me alone!"

That was it. He had been aware all along that a controlling spirit was inside him. He had been living in obedience to Satan and this demon, probably more than just one. Satan was his lord and master. To be free, he must be willing to surrender to Christ, who had the power over Satan to set his captives free from his bondage. The demon must be removed by Jesus through the power of the Holy Spirit.

The man would go no further with the issue. He wanted to leave and keep things just the way they had been when he walked in the door. The four ministers led him out of my office and into their car. They took him back across the state to his cabin in thick woods beside the Mississippi River. I never heard from him again. This account shows that fallen angels are emotional and volitional beings.

Jesus Is Not an Angel

Jesus is not, nor has He ever been, an angel. He created the angels. In New Age literature it is not uncommon to see the claim made that Jesus was an angel when He came to earth or that He is an angel now. This is patently untrue and borders on blasphemy. The Bible makes the distinction:

> But when He again brings the Firstborn into the
>   world, He says,
>   "Let all the angels of God worship Him."
> And of the angels He says,
>   "Who makes His angels spirits
>   and His ministers a flame of fire."
> But to the Son He says:
>   "Your throne, O God, is forever and ever." (Hebrews
>   1:6–8)

It is clear, then, that the Son of God is God the Son, and the angels worship Him. They are creatures, and He is Lord and occupies the throne of heaven eternally.

Two Archangels Are Named in the Bible

An archangel is the highest position among the angelic chain of command. He is a leader, like a general in a modern army. The Scriptures name Lucifer and Michael as archangels. At first, Lucifer was the highest of the two. After he became apostate (see chapter 2) and led the revolt against God and His angelic hosts, Lucifer was cast out of heaven. His absence left the number one position available for Michael, who is now the highest angel and leader of all of God's angels.

Some teach that Gabriel is an archangel, but there is no reference in Scripture to him occupying that position. He is used by God to carry out special assignments involving Israel.

Angels Are Creatures, Not to Be Worshipped

We must never attribute deity to angels or any other creation of God. Some feel that, since angels live in heaven, they should be reverenced just as we reverence God. A created being cannot possess godhood on any level. We must not pray to them or ascribe divine powers to them. In Revelation 22, the apostle John tells us that he was so overcome when he saw and heard the visions that he fell at the feet of the angel who delivered them to him. The angel tersely corrected him:

> Then he said to me, "See that you do not do that. For I am your fellow servant, and of your brethren the prophets, and of those who keep the words of this book. Worship God. (see Revelation 22:8–9)

In Colossians, Paul warns against worshipping angels:

> Let no one cheat you of your reward, taking delight in false humility and worship of angels, intruding into those things which he has not seen, vainly puffed up by his fleshly mind, and not holding fast to the Head, from whom all the body, nourished and knit together by joints and ligaments, grows with the increase that is from God. (Colossians 2:18–19)

Two

THE OCCUPATIONS OF ANGELS

> For by Him were all things created, that are in Heaven and that are on earth, visible and invisible, whether *thrones* or *dominions* or *principalities* or *powers*. All things were created through Him and for Him. (Colossians 1:16, emphasis added)

God the Son created, organized, and equipped the angels. Paul gave us four basic divisions of them. Within each division there could be any number of occupations. The four are thrones, dominions, principalities, and powers. They seem to be listed in a ranking order.

The throne angels are the highest order. They serve around the throne of God and are divided into two classes: *cherubim* and *seraphim*. *Thronos* means rule or administration. The cherubim are assigned to protect God's throne of glory. The attack on God's throne by Satan shows us that cherubim are absolutely necessary to protect the Most High from any intrusion by evil angels. The seraphim are assigned to reflect God's glory through worship and adoration. They are singers and worship leaders. Isaiah's vision of the LORD being worshipped shows us the seraphim at work. They are singing, adoring, hovering, and assisting Isaiah with confession of sin:

> In the year that King Uzziah died, I saw the Lord sitting on a throne, high and lifted up, and the train of His robe filled the temple. Above it stood seraphim; each one had six wings: with two he covered his face, with two he covered his feet, and with two he flew. And one cried to another and said,
>
> "Holy, holy, holy is the LORD of hosts;
>
> The whole earth is full of His glory!" (Isaiah 6:1–3)

The dominion angels are charged with the oversight of other angels. The term is *kuriotes*, meaning "lordship" or "rule." These angels are given gifts of command and leadership.

The principalities angels are given great authority as well. The word *arche*, meaning "first ones," indicates they have an oversight of some kind. This term is used in the Bible for both holy and evil angels.

The powers angels are given authority over whatever situations they are assigned to. With the angels, whatever occupation they are given is an important one. God did not make any indolent angels.

Each of these divisions represents authority on some level. When we consider that millions of angels were created, we can understand why a huge command structure would be necessary, for maximum effectiveness. Jesus Christ, the Son of God, has ultimate rule and leadership over them all (Matthew 28:18).

What Do Angels Do?

Since heaven and the universe are expansive far beyond our knowledge, we can't know everything that angels are assigned to do.

Throughout the Bible, angels are seen taking on various occupations. Some are mentioned below.

Messaging (witnessing). Some angels are given messages by God to deliver to people on earth. The word "angel" means "messenger" in both Testaments. Some examples:

The angel Gabriel was sent to the prophet Daniel with a portion of Scripture giving the number of years of the "times of the Gentiles" and their forced occupation of Jerusalem, from the decree of Artaxerxes of Persia to the close of the great tribulation. Gabriel's journey from Heaven to earth with this crucial prophecy was interrupted by Satan and some of his fallen angels. They attacked Gabriel and held him captive for 21 days, when the archangel Michael overpowered them and set Gabriel free to continue his journey to Daniel. Notice:

> Then he said to me, "Do not fear, Daniel, for from the first day that you set your heart to understand, and to humble yourself before your God, your words were heard; and I have come because of your words. But the prince of the kingdom of Persia withstood me twenty-one days; and behold, Michael, one of the chief princes, came to help me, for I had been left alone there with the kings of Persia." (Daniel 10:12,13)

Gabriel, whose ministry as a messenger of God to Israel is noted in both Testaments, appeared to Mary with the annunciation of Jesus' conception and birth. He later appeared to Elizabeth, a cousin of Mary, who would give birth to John the Baptist (see Luke ch.1).

An angel stood with Paul on a ship sailing to Rome, during a storm (see Acts 27). Throughout the Bible, angels fly from the throne of God with messages to various people.

Worshipping. Led by seraphim, who are the worship leaders of heaven, the angels of God are inspired to worship Him, no matter what their other duties may be: "Let all the angels of God worship Him" (Hebrews 1:6).

Warring. The title, "LORD of hosts" means "LORD of the angelic armies." The hosts of heaven are combat angels, who are led into battle by Michael the archangel. If our eyes were opened to see the spirit world, we would be amazed to see the angelic activity going on all around us. The following passage looks back on the invisible war between God's angels and the evil angels when Lucifer led his dark angels into heaven to overthrow God:

> And war broke out in heaven; Michael and his angels
> fought with the dragon; and the dragon and his angels
> fought, but they did not prevail, nor was a place found
> for them in heaven any longer. (Revelation 12:7–8)

There are many records in the Scriptures that reveal the angels in combat, either in the spiritual world or in the earth.

Working. Angels work for God. Their work can be categorized in at least three ways: expecting, directing, and protecting.

"Expecting," means that angels keep their attention focused, expecting as they wait for His commands. Some angels are assigned to watch over children. Jesus said that they "behold" the face of God, expecting His command to them (Matthew 18:10). An example of their attentiveness to His will is in Genesis 24. An angel went with Abraham's servant on a journey to find a wife for Isaac, Abraham's son. He expected God to lead him to her and to reveal her to him.

Angels "directing" are used to show people directions, choices, or commands. An angel appeared to Gideon to direct him to Israel's enemies (Numbers 20:16). An angel assisted with the cleansing of Joshua the high priest (Zechariah 3:5). Two angels were dispatched to the tomb of Jesus to roll away the stone, reveal to the women that He had risen from the dead, and direct them to tell Peter and the other apostles that He was alive (Luke 24:1–12).

Angels "protecting" are ministries often found in the Bible. An angel was sent to protect Daniel when he was thrown into a den of lions. He shut the mouths of the lions to save the prophet's life (Daniel 6:16–24). Gabriel informed Mary and Joseph that Herod was searching to find the Baby to kill Him and counseled them to take Him into Egypt until

Herod was dead; an angel also let them know when it was safe to return home (Matthew 2:13–20). A popular and precious passage about angelic protection is in Psalm 91:

> He shall give His angels charge over you,
> to keep you in all your ways.
> In their hands they shall bear you up,
> lest you dash your foot against a stone. (Psalm 91:11–12)

Part of the working ministry of angels includes their protection of all whom the Lord designates to receive special angelic oversight. This is usually because the Lord has a special purpose for that person to fill or because prevailing prayer has been offered up for him or her. An example that I became aware of, first-hand, is given in the following story.

Angel Impersonates Israeli Soldier

The following account was related to me when I was preaching in Nazareth, Israel, in the fall of 1973. The Yom Kippur war had been raging in Israel, especially in northern Galilee. I was preaching in the Nazareth Baptist Church, which operated a school. Its principal was a brother of the pastor of the church. He related a tearful story to me about an angel who posed as an Israeli soldier to save him from a firing squad, in a case of mistaken identity.

Members of an Israeli patrol discovered the principal in an off-limits area. They assumed that he was spying for the Syrians and refused to believe that he had made a wrong turn while going toward the city. He was arrested and taken to a stockade. He was told that he was scheduled to be shot as a spy the following morning.

He spent the night in prayer, asking the Lord to spare his life because he was innocent of the charges. The following morning at six o'clock, a soldier with an Uzi slung over his shoulder, came to take him to the execution area. He was to be tied to a post, blindfolded, and shot.

As the two of them approached the gate to the killing area, he could see the post where his life would end. The soldier led him past the gate and down a road which led out of the encampment. No other soldier seemed to notice them as they passed the gate, then past the stockade. His fear increased. What different punishment had they devised for him? Were they going to trade him to the Syrians for an Israeli prisoner? As he walked, he cried and prayed.

Walking south, he could see Nazareth in the distance. As they approached a small rise in the roadway, the soldier ordered him to stop and look straight ahead. The soldier resumed his place behind the principal and said again, "Walk!"

The school principal soon became aware that he was alone. He heard no footsteps and saw no shadow of the soldier. He broke the rules and turned around. There were no trees nor brush that his captor could be hiding behind. Was someone going to shoot him in the back from a distance? Slowly, the realization washed over him. He was alone, free, and on his way home. The Israeli soldier had vanished into thin air! His footsteps quickened. In ten minutes or so, he was entering the outskirts of his hometown. He ran to the school and found faculty and students praying for him.

As he told me the story, he wept and praised the Lord. A genuine miracle of deliverance had been worked to save his life. He never hesitated to tell me that the soldier was an angel of God who had carried out a Psalm 91 assignment on his behalf. He had wanted to thank him, but he was long gone back to heaven. Angels leave no calling cards. They expect no tips or accolades. Praise belongs to Jesus. With an angel, it is enough that his mission has been fulfilled.

Some Special Operations of Angels

The Scriptures give us examples of special operations or designations of angels at times. Here are some of them.

The Angel of the Lord. This use of the word *angel* in this way is sometimes confusing, but it designates a special operation of God. The term is used only in the Old Testament and seems to identify God Himself taking an angelic form for a special reason. Many scholars call the appearance a "theophany," which means a manifestation of God, either in a visual or auditory form. In Judges 13 He appeared to Manoah and his wife in answer to a prayer of Manoah. Manoah didn't know who He was, however, until He disappeared in the flames of a sacrifice.

Another such appearance was to Moses in the flames of a burning bush (Exodus 3). Often, the person being addressed by the Angel of the Lord recognizes His deity and seeks to worship Him. In Numbers 22, He appears to Balaam's donkey and later, to Balaam himself. In whatever situation He appears, it is God using the form of an angel as a way of approaching a human. In such an appearance, He is the "Divine Messenger."

Chariots of Fire. In the Bible, fire is used to symbolize judgment or else to refine one's character through persecution. Chariots were often used for military conveyance by powerful armies. The horses and chariots of fire, such as we see in 2 Kings 6, were visible expressions of God's warring angels. The Ethiopian treasurer of the court of the Queen of Ethiopia, to whom Philip was ordered to speak, was riding in a chariot (Acts 8), so we can assume that they were also used for transportation if one could afford them.

The Angels of the Churches in Revelation 2 and 3. The seven letters to churches in Asia Minor were each addressed to an "angel." For most of my ministry I have considered these angels to be the pastors or leading elders of the churches. The more I study angels in the Bible, however, the more I am convinced that they might be just what they are called: angels. Briefly, let me give reasons.

First, if they were human leaders of the churches, why are they called angels? Second, they are represented by seven stars in the right hand of Jesus, and stars often represent angels. Third, to say that they are pastors or elders, and in Christ's hand, would mean that His authority rests with the human leader of each church. What if the pastor or elder becomes corrupt? Does this mean that they would get that way while under His authority? Fourth, John uses the word *elder* elsewhere, such as in chapter 4. Why not here? To call them what the text calls them, "angels," would mean that Christ has assigned an angel to be His overseer and protector of each church.

Admittedly, there is also good evidence for assuming the angels to be humans. One explanation would be that they were men sent by each church to visit John and give him a report of these churches and find out his condition, since he was in his late nineties. This one doesn't resonate with me. It is true that the messages to the churches were addressed to the "angel" of each church, and it seems that it means the human leader. I will leave this knot to be untied by the reader. Are these angels human leaders of the churches, or God's angels?

The Four Living Creatures (KJV: the four beasts). In Revelation chapter 4, John saw the throne of God in heaven and twenty-four thrones around it. Accompanying the thrones were "four living creatures". They also appear in Ezekiel 1 and again in Ezekiel 10 and are called "cherubim," which are throne angels who protect the throne of God. They carry a platform of some kind and are identified as "wheels" having eyes and four faces. The shekinah glory is above them, which is the presence of God.

These are four special cherubim who are responsible for the transport and protection of the Most High. Each had four faces and four wings. One face was that of a man, the second a lion, the third an ox, and the fourth face was that of an eagle. Their color was like burning coals of fire, with lightning flashing out of them.

These are not "beasts," as translated in the King James translation. They are angels, the most powerful and honored of the throne angels. They are creatures, made by the Son of God back before time began. We will meet them in Heaven.

We move our attention now to Lucifer's rebellion and his creation of sin by obeying his arrogant pride instead of our glorious, eternal God.

THE REBELLION OF LUCIFER

How you are fallen from heaven,
O Lucifer, son of the morning! (Isaiah 14:12)

Lucifer, the highest archangel, was created with all other angels by the Son of God. Before time and the present universe came into existence, he instigated an overthrow of God and heaven and was defeated. Jesus told the seventy disciples about it when He sent them on a preaching mission: "And He said to them, 'I saw Satan fall like lightning from heaven'" (Luke 10:18).

A war raged in heaven between the good angels and the evil angels. The result was the defeat of the rebel angels and their expulsion from heaven (Revelation 12:7–9). The Son of God was involved in the battle since He is God the Second Person. This happened before He came into the world. At least a third of the angels joined Lucifer and were also banished from the face of God (Revelation 12:4).

The prophets Isaiah and Ezekiel have given us details about the reason Lucifer organized the attempted coup. Ezekiel gave a prophecy against world powers that were being used by God to discipline Judah for her sins. He called him the "king of Tyre," in the prophecy (see Ezekiel 28:12–19).

The characteristics of the king of Tyre are those of Lucifer, who was an archangel. He was one of the cherubim. In fact, he was the highest cherub and the highest of all the angels. More than that, he was the highest of all creatures after the universe was made. He was in Eden (v 13). He had walked up and down on the "stones of fire" on the holy mountain of God. These were brilliant gemstones that we would call precious stones. They reflected the glory of God and looked as though fire was coming out of them. Lucifer was free to move around the garden of Eden, having the authority of an administrator and executive. He is called the "covering angel." Other cherubim carried the throne of God, but Lucifer was exalted to the place of honor to be above Him as His protecting angel.

Lucifer was the epitome of perfection. He lacked nothing when God created him. His intellect, makeup, morality, abilities, and position were complete. Morally, Lucifer was the highest in credibility and judgment, until his pride took him down. He was the "seal" of perfection, perfect in his ways. No creature had been so complete, nor had any been given such power and prestige. Not only was he God's covering angel, but he was placed on earth before Adam was created to be its administrator. He had all of heaven and earth as well. Eden teemed with everything beautiful and inspiring. It was garnished with precious stones, metals, and minerals:

> Every precious stone was your covering:
> the sardius, topaz, and diamond,
> beryl, onyx and jasper,
> sapphire, turquoise, and emerald with gold. (Ezekiel 28:13)

This description hints at Lucifer's weakness. He became infatuated with himself. He was adorned with the beautiful, the precious, and the most expensive coverings. Among the angels, the arts flourished in that pristine setting. The music that Lucifer created and played was the most inspiring that angel ears could hear.

The workmanship of your timbrels and pipes
was prepared for you on the day you were created.
(Ezekiel 28:13)

From the day he was created he possessed the scores, the instruments, the perfect melodies and harmonies—all that was needed to provide music for God Himself, Father, Son, and Holy Spirit. Lucifer's music came right out of his very being. He could create instruments without needing anyone else. As the praise and worship leader of heaven, he had all the gifts for creating the music that expressed glory to God. All of this and much more was his. He had everything, but he wanted more, and he felt that he deserved more. He did not want to create music by which to worship God. He wanted to be god and create music for his own worship.

His name says it all. *Lucifer* means "son of the morning" (Isaiah 14:12) or "shining one". It is sometimes translated "bright morning star."

The Fall of Lucifer

At some point in eternity past, God's highest and brightest, most authoritative archangel conspired to lead an overthrow of the kingdom of God, which now includes the present universe. It is important to know why and how it happened, because our sin follows the same pattern as Lucifer's rebellion. Ezekiel records God's statement to Lucifer following the attempted coup and its failure:

Your heart was lifted up because of your beauty;
you corrupted your wisdom for the sake of your splendor;
I cast you to the ground,
I laid you before kings,
that they might gaze at you. (Ezekiel 28:17)

The rebellion began as Lucifer fawned over his own beauty, wisdom, authority, and power. The more he "looked at himself in the mirror," to use an old cliché, the more he came to believe that he could get most of the angels to join him in a revolt, because they surely would prefer him over God. They could stage a coup d'état, take over heaven and earth, and run things like they wanted to. He could be the god of all things by dispossessing the Creator. Five times he said in his heart, as he worked through his plan, "I will." Isaiah records these musings of his ego:

> How you are fallen from heaven,
> O Lucifer, son of the morning!
> How you are cut down to the ground,
> you who weakened the nations!
> For you have said in your heart:
> "I will ascend into heaven,
> I will exalt my throne above the stars of God;
> I will also sit on the mount of the congregation
> on the farthest sides of the north;
> I will ascend above the heights of the clouds;
> I will be like the Most High."
> Yet you shall be brought down to Sheol,
> to the lowest depths of the pit. (Isaiah 14:12–15)

In a notation concerning this passage, C.I. Scofield observed, "When Lucifer said, 'I will,' sin began." Pride, coupled with self-will, propelled Lucifer to commit the greatest act of rebellion ever known. His ambition was enormous. He determined that he would have the glory of God for himself by ascending to the heavenly throne. It would become his own; then he would be exalted above the stars—all the angels. He would take command of heaven's armies and threaten the angels who refused to join him in the revolt.

Everything God had created, Lucifer coveted. It all had already been promised to the Son of God, as written in the Psalms:

> I will declare the decree:
> The Lord has said to Me,
> "You are My Son,

today I have begotten You.
Ask of Me and I will give You
the nations for Your inheritance,
and the ends of the earth for Your possession." (Psalm
2:7–8)

Now we can understand why Lucifer hates the Son of God and has
repeatedly tried to kill Him. If the Father fulfills the terms of the Davidic
Covenant as is declared in the verses above and Psalm 89, it means that
Jesus Christ will be established as the King of all creation and Lord of
heaven and earth. It means that Lucifer is finished when Jesus returns
from heaven to earth.

How Sin Began

Sin began with Lucifer. As we read his musings within himself, that
he would be "like God", we remember that it is specifically this same
ambition that Satan promised to Eve:

> Then the serpent said to the woman, "You will not
> surely die. For God knows that in the day you eat of
> it your eyes will be opened, and you will be like God,
> knowing good and evil." (Genesis 3:4–5)

We can also understand the meaning of Satan's third temptation of
Jesus, when he offered Jesus all the kingdoms of the world if He would
acknowledge him (Satan) to be god:

> Again, the devil took Him up on an exceedingly high
> mountain, and showed Him all the kingdoms of the
> world and their glory. And he said to Him, "All these
> things will I give You if You will fall down and worship
> me." (Matthew 4:8–9)

The devil had tried a military overthrow of heaven to oust God and become "like God." That failed, so he began a campaign of trickery and deceit to have it. He also tried repeatedly to kill Jesus before He went to the cross. Then, as Jesus hung helplessly and in terrible pain and weakness on the cross, Satan and his demon horde put maximum pain and suffering on Him, believing that they could surely kill Him there. That also failed, as we shall see later.

Satan's consummate goal is to be worshipped like God. He gets maximum ego satisfaction when we give in to his temptations. To accomplish this goal, he launches his "big three" motivators at us: the world, the flesh, and the devil. He has an all-consuming ego that will eventually destroy him.

The core of the first sin, committed by Adam and Eve who were tricked by the serpent, which was Satan in the form of a beautiful creature, was to disobey God and eat of the tree of the knowledge of good and evil. In disobeying God's command not to eat of it, they made themselves their own gods. They did their own will instead of God's. The serpent's temptation stimulated their pride and activated their egos.

God had shown them that He would make the rules of morality. The tree of knowledge of good and evil was a standing parable, in the very center of life in the garden. It showed them that their Creator reserved the right to establish what is good and what is evil. They had perfect freedom, with that one exception. They were not capable of making up the rules that governed moral thinking and behavior, because their pride would always favor their will over God's will.

When we decide to say, "I will" instead of "Thy will," we reproduce Lucifer's rebellion. We mount a personal rebellion against the Lord every time we deny Him His rightful place as lawgiver, judge, and determiner of truth.

How the Rebellion Ended

Only one outcome could be expected when Lucifer mounted the invasion of heaven. He was defeated and deposed, thrown out of heaven along with the angels who followed him. He was sent into outer space and into the atmosphere of earth. As Jesus said, "I saw Satan fall like lightning from heaven" (Luke 10:18).

In that passage from Luke, Jesus had sent out seventy disciples to evangelize the area. He wanted them to understand that Satan had no authority over them, but they had authority over him. When they returned from the evangelistic campaign, they reported that even the demons were subject to them in His name. He told them that He had seen Satan's fall. He is a fallen creature, who must obey the Son of God. Every saint has authority over him in Jesus's name.

How Did Lucifer Recruit Other Angels?

How was the archangel Lucifer able to convince about a third of the angels to join him in an overthrow of God and heaven? Consider the prestige Lucifer enjoyed among the other angels. He was the highest of the archangels and of all the angels. He was the most illustrious creature ever designed by God. He was a cherub, a throne angel, and held the unique position of being "the anointed cherub that covers." This means that it was Lucifer who was God's choice for being His covering angel. Four cherubim transported the throne of God. The covering angel flew over the Most High, forming protection and providing a canopy of beauty over Him.

Enter Michael

The rebellion and fall of Lucifer caused a change in angelic leadership. We notice that Satan's attitude toward Michael became competitive, perhaps hostile. This sometimes happens when a leader is replaced by his second-in-command. A conflict between them arose over the issue of the burial of Moses's body. It appears that Lucifer, now Satan, tried to select an alternate spot for the interment. We are not told in Scripture why it mattered. He had been the chief archangel. Something about

Moses's body apparently had been under his jurisdiction until he was deposed. He still wanted to be in charge of the burial place, which the Lord had determined at first.

We can get a feel for the tension between the two angels as we read a statement by Judah, a half-brother of Jesus:

> Yet Michael the archangel, in contending with the devil, when he disputed about the body of Moses, dared not bring against him a reviling accusation, but said, "The Lord rebuke you!" (Jude 9)

The Lord apparently had chosen the place where He wanted Moses's body buried, but Satan wanted another place. We don't know where nor why, but a safe bet is that it had something to do with his inflated ego. Michael stopped him from disobeying God. However, it is possible that Michael took the issue straight to God, which ended the argument. Moses was buried in a secret place.

When Jesus took Peter, James, and John with Him to the top of a high mountain and allowed them to see Him transfigured, they reportedly saw Jesus talking with Moses and Elijah (see Mark 9:2–8). Even in his spiritual body, Moses looked like himself without his physical body, which had been secreted somewhere in a valley in the land of Moab (Deuteronomy 34:5–6).

What Effect Did Lucifer's Rebellion Have on the Angels Who Rebelled?

The characteristics of movement and personhood (intellect, emotions, will) were not affected. They were still able to fly and do things that angels were given the natural ability to do. The effect was moral. They became evil, through and through, without any qualities of goodness. They still had a will, but it turned dark. They now *will* to do wickedness. They use their God-given capabilities against God and godliness. Their intellects and emotions now gravitate only toward what is bad. If I may use the contrasting colors of white and black to illustrate the morality of the rebelling angels, they all became deep black whereas they first were created a brilliant white. Even Lucifer's name changed to match his evil heart: His name now is Satan, meaning "adversary." He and his cohorts are adversaries to God and His people. Here are some of their characteristics.

They are rebellious.

They knew God and knew that He had created them. When they learned of Lucifer's plan to overthrow Him, they knew it was sheer anarchy. However, they were accustomed to Lucifer's leadership and influence, and their closeness to him made the decision to join him much easier. They became rebels and cohorts with Lucifer's act of high treason.

They are restless.

Jesus gave an example of a man who had been possessed, and after the demon was removed from him, he became very restless.

> When the unclean spirit is gone out of a man he walks through dry places, seeking rest and finding none. Then he says, "I will return to my house from which I came." And when he comes, he finds it empty, swept and put in order. Then he goes and takes with him seven other spirits more wicked than himself, and they enter and dwell there; and the last state of that man is worse than the first. So shall it also be with this wicked generation. (Matthew 12:43–45)

This teaching by Jesus provides valuable information about demon possession that we should read carefully.

First, demon possession is not a psychological malady, although it may produce problems of the mind. It is not insanity, although it may cause insanity. Satan tried to possess heaven and all of God's domain. He was not allowed to do it. However, he and his angels can enter into human lives and possess them.

Demons can enter unsaved people if their will becomes weak and they put up little or no resistance. They dwell in the spirit, and, since spirit and soul are joined, they will affect the mind (soul, personality, thinking) as well. When they gain this level of control, they can cause all kinds of physical illness and disability. We must be careful not to assume that all physical or mental illness is caused by demons. This is not the case. The demon's purpose is to control the person, cause pain and suffering, and eventually kill him/her.

In the passage above, the "house" represents the spirit of the man where the demon lives. Being "empty, swept and put in order" describes a moral reformation, but no regeneration of the spirit. "Seven" speaks of completeness. The demon that was cast out came back with enough others to overcome the effects of the new morality. The man is in bondage again, but this time, instead of having one demon to be exorcised, now there are eight.

I once counseled a woman who had symptoms of possession, although she said she was a Christian. A lady staff member and I worked with her nine hours. We encountered intense resistance before nineteen demons finally left her through the power of the Holy Spirit. As each one was discovered, I commanded it to give its name and wrote it down. After she was completely free, we gave her the complete gospel. Her will was then at liberty to receive Jesus as her Savior and Lord without interference from Satan's power.

They are ruthless.

Dark angels will not hesitate to destroy a human life. They are utterly selfish. Young or old, rich or poor, educated or illiterate, male or female, even children and babies can be inhabited by demons if they can find a way to enter. When we think of a demon, we must scratch our conception of fallen angels as mischievous little cherubs. Each is more wicked than another. They will use a person's life and resources to gratify their lusts and please their master. Scripture gives us examples of their ruthlessness, like this one:

A Legion of Demons That Drove A Man Insane

A legion of demons entered a man at Gadara and drove him insane by creating life situations for him that worried, threatened, and hurt him constantly. He lived in caves that were being used as tombs on a hillside bordering the eastern coast of Lake Galilee. He went naked, cut himself with sharp stones, and leaped about, screaming (Mark 5:1–20). The "strong man" or leader of the large number of dark angels called itself "Legion." A legion of Roman soldiers was 6,800 infantry and cavalry. There must have been about that number of demons inhabiting the man's spiritual capacity and controlling his body and mind. Imagine living in a house with thousands of lunatics, violent sex offenders, and criminally insane, homicidal maniacs running loose, and all bent on hurting or killing you. Would such conditions make you suicidal? His heart was a literal madhouse. The following account also demonstrates ruthlessness.

A Ruthless Demon, More Powerful Than Nine Disciples

One demon, not six thousand, had entered a teenage boy. This one had often driven the boy to attempt suicide. This account is in Mark 9:14–29. Jesus had left nine of his disciples in the village where the boy's family lived, while He took Peter, James, and John with Him to the top of a mountain. He was transfigured before them, meaning that He allowed the glory of His deity to shine through His humanity. It was visual proof that He was God the Son.

Down in the village the other nine found themselves being approached by the boy's father, who desperately begged them to cast the demon out of him, but they lacked the power to do it. When Jesus and the three returned, the father appealed to Him, telling Him that the nine disciples were not able to do it. The demon was powerful, causing the boy to attempt suicide by jumping into the fire or water. Dark angels desire to hurt and destroy the people in whom they reside. Jesus expelled the demon, but as it left the boy's body, it caused him to have a violent seizure. Jesus told the disciples they were not able to remove the demon because "this kind" could not be expelled except by prayer and fasting.

They Are Reprobate.

In the Bible, a *reprobate* is someone who professes faith in Christ yet lives a life that dishonors or denies Him (Romans 1:28). The fallen angels had once known godliness. They lived in heaven, the abode of God. Since they no longer wanted Him in their knowledge, but preferred to obey the fallen archangel, Lucifer, they fell into the lowest depths of corruption. Fallen angels are totally depraved, though they once served God and joined in praise and worship of His glorious Being. Demons have no redeeming moral nor social qualities. They are worthless beings who only work evil. Only hell awaits their presence. (See Matthew 5:41.)

They Are Repulsive.

People in deliverance ministries have learned how unclean, deceitful, and vicious the demons are. They are inveterate liars. The Bible calls them "unclean" and "lying" spirits. I have heard them utter filthy language in conversation and scream obscenities at me when I commanded them to give their name. More than this, they blaspheme God when they become angry because their lies are exposed. They will do almost anything to avoid giving their names or leaving the people they have inhabited. When counseling sessions are over, I am exhausted, and I feel filthy because I have been in the presence of utterly depraved creatures who hate me.

They Are Retaliatory.

When evil angels are expelled from human lives, they tend to retaliate, to "get even" or to express their hatred and anger in some graphic way. They want to hurt their victims one last time as they leave. In Mark's account of the boy in the village at the foot of the mountain, the demon that was exorcised was furious at having to leave and, even in the presence of the Son of God, vented his rage with a loud scream and causing paroxysmal pain, almost killing the boy.

> When Jesus saw that the people came running together, He rebuked the unclean spirit, saying to it: "Deaf and dumb spirit, I command you, come out of him and enter him no more!" Then the spirit cried out, convulsed him greatly, and came out of him. And he became as one dead, so that many said, "He is dead." But Jesus took him by the hand and lifted him up, and he arose. (Mark 9:25–27)

Note that the Greek word for "cried" is *krazo*. It means a loud, shrilling sound, such as a crow makes. It also is used for a screaming cry for revenge. "Convulsed" is from the Greek word *sparasso,* meaning "to tear." Before the demon left the child's body, it caused a violent convulsion and cried out with a hideous shriek. It was an act of retaliation, and Mark uses the language that best conveys the graphic violence of the event. Demons subscribe to Satan's philosophy of "rule or ruin."

They Are Realists.

I believe fallen angels are realists. They did not lose their memory when they became evil by following Lucifer. They know what the Scriptures say about their future, that they will one day be confined to hell, the lake of fire. They recognize the deity and lordship of Jesus, that He has absolute authority in heaven and earth (Luke 4:34). When they are commanded in Jesus's name to leave a person, they must do so, but they will often make the process as difficult as they can by repeatedly refusing to come out, or hurting their victim in some way. We Christians must expect to bear Satan's lashes before we hear Michael's trumpet call.

They Can Reinvent Themselves.

All angels can take on temporary forms that are visible to humans. The anecdote given earlier about an angel of God taking on the temporary likeness of an Israeli soldier to save the life of an Arab school principal is a good example. Throughout the Bible we sometimes encounter angels reinventing themselves as a way of accomplishing a task given to them by God. They can look and act like humans and fulfill God's directions perfectly.

Dark angels also have this capability. The apostle Paul spoke about Satan's ability to take on characteristics of an angel of God:

> For such are false apostles, deceitful workers, transforming themselves into apostles of Christ. And no wonder! For Satan himself transforms himself into an angel of light. (2 Corinthians 11:13–14)

Satan also took the likeness of a beautiful animal (at the time), a serpent, when he deceived Eve (Genesis 3:1–6). The Antichrist will take on the appealing traits of a handsome, godly, benevolent peacemaker and will deceive most of the world.

Even though fallen angels can reinvent themselves, most of them satisfy their need to deceive humans through demon possession rather than by taking various forms. By entering a human's spirit, they can control the person. If the demon-possessed person has influence over other people, large groups can be deceived. I believe Adolf Hitler was under the control of demons. He became one of the world's most evil dictators and was responsible for the suffering and death of millions of people.

They Frequently Relate to Idols.

Fallen angels relate hand-in-glove to idols. The idol can be crafted and carried around or hung on a wall or on furniture. In Western culture, an idol can be a person, picture, or practice, especially on TV or in the movies. Whatever takes the place of God is an idol. The first of the Ten Commandments forbids all idols (Exodus 20:3–6).

> Professing themselves to be wise, they became fools, and changed the glory of the incorruptible God into an image made like corruptible man—and birds and four-footed animals and creeping things. (Romans 1:22–23)

Leave the Idols Alone

The apostle Paul warned us, to flee from idolatry (1 Corinthians 10:14), and the apostle John told us to stay away from idols (1 John 5:21). I have encountered demonic idolatry in pagan forms in places like Haiti, Africa, and Brazil. In my first preaching mission overseas, in a church, of all places, I purchased an idol which was used in religious ceremonies. I mentioned to a missionary friend that I wanted to take it back home with me to show members of my church. He warned me not to carry it home with me but to leave it alone. When I asked "why?" he told me that demons were associated with them, and if I possessed an idol, its demons would oppress me, my family, or people in my congregation who handled it.

A Japanese college student came to me for counseling. She was being threatened at night by a dark form that hovered over her and choked her. She could not think clearly and dreaded being alone. I asked her if she was raised a Buddhist. "Yes," she said. "I still am a Buddhist." I asked her if she had seen a physician and the school counselor. They had given her drugs to make her sleep, but they had not helped with the fearful darkness that intimidated her at night. I asked her if she had a Buddha in her room. Her reply was that her mother had given her three of them before she left for America. She had a paper one, a cardboard one, and a small wooden one. She had one in her purse, one in her car, and one in her dorm room.

When I told her that evil spirits were associated with the idols, she began to cry. She said she could never give them up because her mother had made them for her. She asked me to excuse her. She left and I did not see her again for two weeks. The problem became so acute she came to see me again. I told her that she must receive Christ as her Savior and Lord to get victory over the fearful attacker. She said that she would become a Christian if she could also keep her Buddhas. I said, "No. Jesus will not share you with an idol. You must get rid of them."

She cried again. Her trembling little hand reached into her briefcase, pulled the three Buddhas out, and handed them to me. I had to tell her "No" again. "They do not belong to me. They are yours. You must give them up." I suggested that we go down to the back side of our church parking lot and build a fire. Then she could give them up to the fire. As we walked, she cried. I gathered sticks and built a small fire. We prayed. I asked Jesus to hear her prayer. She had a difficult time with a short little prayer.

She placed the paper idol into the flames. I began hearing an outcry, faint at first, coming out of the fire. When she placed the cardboard Buddha, then the wooden one, into the fire, the outcry became louder. She was frightened and I was astonished. Such a thing had never happened when I was counseling. Then, a miracle occurred. When the last idol had been destroyed, her fear and tears left her face. She looked at me and said, "I am free!"

Back in my office, she prayed to receive Jesus as her Savior and surrendered to His Lordship over her life. Since her will had been set free, she could honestly and completely become a born-again Christian.

Many and perhaps most idols have demons attached to them. They must be totally surrendered before true regeneration can take place. This is true of any form of idolatry.

Conclusion

All the angels who joined Lucifer in the great angelic rebellion are our mortal and eternal enemies. They are now known as "demons". Our constant battle with them demands that we know how they are organized and equipped for warfare against us.

Four

SPIRITUAL RECONNAISSANCE: KNOW YOUR ENEMY

Reconnaissance is the investigation and discovery of vital information about an enemy army with a view to defeating them in battle. It is an indispensable operation. Sun Tzu, the Chinese general of the sixth century BC, whose battle strategies have been studied by military professionals for centuries, said, "If you know your enemy and know yourself, you need not fear a hundred battles" (*The Art of War*. Goodreads, Quotes from Sun Tzu).

In this chapter, we will study a reconnaissance report from Paul the apostle. He shows us how Satan's immense hosts are divided among an "elaborately organized hierarchy" (Unger, *Biblical Demonology*) of dark angels who control them and who are charged with fulfilling his "schemes." As we translate the Greek words, they are, *the first ones, the authorities, the world powers of this darkness,* and *the spiritual forces of evil in the heavens* (Ephesians 6:12).

My military service was in the reconnaissance battalion of an armored division. I was a tank commander. Our job was to encounter the enemy in unexpected thrusts and probe his forward units to find his strong and weak points, estimate his troop strengths and weapons, and get the information to our division command. This enabled our tanks and infantry to engage the enemy wisely and in force.

We know the nature and organizational schemes of Satan's army. We must not attempt to defeat them, however, unless we also know ourselves. Since we do not struggle against human devices but against invisible, spiritual forces of evil, we must ask ourselves if we are spiritually ready for the battle. The answer depends on the condition of our weapons, called the "whole armor of God" (Ephesians 6:11). In the Greek language of the New Testament, it is one word: *panoplia,* translated, "all the weapons." The Roman soldier's *panoplia* included shield, breastplate, sword, lance, helmet, and sandals or boots with hobnails for traction. For the Christian soldier who is facing combat with an invisible, invincible, super-intelligent spiritual foe, there must be armor protecting every place the enemy might strike us and powerful enough to defeat him in spite of whatever method he uses against us.

In my football days, our coaches devised a practice exercise called "the bull ring". They drew a circle seven or eight feet in diameter; then each lineman took his turn inside it. He had to be strong enough to stay in the circle, crouched in position. When the coach blew his whistle, each of the others could rush in and try to knock him off his feet or out of the ring. The man inside had to crouch, plant his cleats into the soil, square his shoulders, and try to survive without being knocked out. Most often, the loser was knocked off his feet, and that was why he lost. Paul prefaces his description of the hierarchy of hell by saying,

> Put on the whole armor of God, that you may be able
> to stand against the wiles of the devil …. Therefore take
> up the whole armor of God, that you may be able to
> withstand in the evil day, and having done all, to stand.
> (Ephesians 6:11,13)

We must stay on our feet, and when the battle is over, we must still be standing inside the ring. We cannot win by our own strength. We understand why we need God's armor when we discover the strengths and strategies of Satan's organization. I call it "The Hierarchy of Hell."

The Hierarchy of Hell

Martin Luther wrote,

> Did we in our own strength confide,
> Our striving would be losing;
> Were not the right Man on our side,
> The Man of God's own choosing.

These lines are taken from an English translation of Martin Luther's 1527 hymn, "A Mighty Fortress Is Our God." I visited the Wartburg Castle in Germany, where Luther was placed under house arrest for his protection from religious enemies who planned to place him on trial for his life. The little apartment-like area where he lived was impressive, not for its décor but for its sparseness. He scratched his name in the thick glass window of one of the rooms. He knew that he was up against enemies so powerful that he could not hope to be victorious over them if he depended on himself alone.

As with Martin Luther, our source of spiritual power is the Lord. He makes His abode within the regenerated spiritual nature of every believer through the presence of the Holy Spirit and enables the risen life of Christ to be lived out in us, including the power of His resurrection. The Holy Spirit is God, the Third Person.

Why will it take God Himself to empower our spiritual combat in our invisible war with Satan? Paul tells us: "Put on the whole armor of God, that you may be able to stand against the wiles of the devil" (Ephesians 6:11). Paul gives three reasons why we cannot win over Satan by our own strength and resolve:

The Devil's Wiles (Strategies)

The "wiles" of the Devil are his strategies for defeating us. The first one is a Greek word, *methodeia*. It means "strategies" or "methods." No matter what methods we devise to win over sin and Satan, he is 'way ahead of us. He can outthink, out-plan, and outfight us every time unless we depend on the power of God's Spirit. The apostle Paul, as strong a Christian as he was, had to admit the failure of his own flesh to defeat sin in his life: "I know that in me (that is, in my flesh) nothing good dwells; for to will is present with me, but how to perform what is good I do not find" (Romans 7:18).

Paul testified that he WAs not able to defeat the sin nature that was in him. No matter how he planned or what he tried, his sin nature kept him defeated. Satan knew exactly what buttons to push, so to speak, to defeat him. A few verses later, however, he gave us the way to victory over Satan and sin: "Jesus Christ our Lord" (Romans 7:25).

Demons cannot read our minds or know our thoughts. Only God can do that. However, fallen angels have a modus operandi on us. They have observed us throughout our lives, to know what we will do in most situations. They know us better than we know ourselves. Never underestimate them. Their strategies against us are well served with information they can use against us.

Our Mortal Struggle

In our central passage, Ephesians 6, Paul says that our struggle against Satan and our sin nature is a fight to the death. It is a second reason why we cannot defeat them alone.

> For we do not wrestle against flesh and blood, but against principalities, against powers, against the rulers of the darkness of this age, against spiritual hosts of wickedness in the heavenly places. (Ephesians 6:12)

When we engage the enemy in combat, we are up against a *spiritual* enemy, not human flesh. The war is an invisible one and the combat is a mortal one. The word he uses, translated "wrestle," is *pale*, pronounced "pay-lay." It was used to describe the mortal combat of two Roman gladiators who fought to the death before a high official and a bloodthirsty crowd. When one subdued the other, he would hold him down, often with his foot on the defeated soldier's neck. He would then look up to the box where the Roman official and his entourage were seated. The official would signal to him, either with a thumbs-up or a thumbs-down. If he allowed the defeated man to live, it was thumbs-up. However, at the discretion of the official and the will of the crowd, he could have his eyes gouged out. Thumbs-down meant death. That was what the screaming crowd came to see. The winner plunged his dagger or sword into the loser's chest, or else put him in a wrestling hold that enabled him to break the man's neck.

The world does not want us to live. It screams for our failure from sin. The devil sets out to defeat us every time, so that we lose our testimony, family, or even our life. We certainly lose our crown. We are in an invisible war, struggling against dark spirit beings who are much more intelligent and powerful than we are and who have the resources of the world to use against our faith in Christ. Demons are invisible to our sight and invincible to our puny human methods. Our struggle will end in certain failure unless we depend on our Savior's resurrection power to defeat Satan's resources.

The Command Structure of Hell's Hierarchy

A third reason why we cannot defeat the devil in our own strength are the enemy combatants we struggle against. Paul says that Satan's army of fallen angels is structured to employ four command groups. There are teeming multitudes of fallen angels who sided with Satan. He divided them into four separate commands. The mission of each command is found in the meaning of the term Paul uses. We know they are separate commands because Paul divides them by using the word "against" to preface each one.

The Principalities. The Greek term is *arche,* pronounced "ar-kay." It means "first ones." These demons make up the operations command. They are the first of the four, the top generals in the devil's army. They answer to him. They are in authority over their command groups.

Incidentally, this term is also used for the hosts of God. His angels have a supreme commander, who is the Lord Jesus. The first of their "first ones" is Michael, the archangel. Apparently, when the revolt was organized by Satan, some of the highest-ranking angels chose to defect and go with him to overthrow the Lord. These are now in the same rank in the devil's army.

The Powers. This word in the original is *exousia,* pronounced "eks-ou-see-ah." It means "rule" or "authority" over other angels. These would likely be the combat command demons. Again, there are many of them. They are in authority over units of their assigned group. These are very powerful demons who train and command others to do their work of deception and possession of people and resources. I cannot know this for sure, but the Bible implies that teams of demons often take over a person, or an organization, or a power source in a strategic entity, like a family, or a business, or a political group.

I have already mentioned the account in Mark 9, but it illustrates this kind of demon leader. While Jesus was on the mount of transfiguration with Peter, James, and John, the other nine disciples waited for them in a village at the foot of the mountain. The father of a teenage boy who had epilepsy and frequent seizures asked them to cast a demon out of him. The demon was destroying his son. The nine attempted an exorcism yet could not expel the demon.

When the Lord returned to the village, the father of the boy rushed to Him and said:

> "I brought You my son, who has a mute spirit. And whenever it seizes him, it throws him down; he foams at the mouth, gnashes his teeth, and becomes rigid. So

I spoke to Your disciples, that they should cast it out,
but they could not." (Mark 9:17–18)

Jesus called for faith from the father and then expelled the demon.
When it came out of the boy, it caused him to have a violent convulsion
so powerful it almost killed him. Jesus, however, took the boy by the
hand and commanded him to get up, which he did. He was free of the
demon and cured of epilepsy. The nine disciples later asked him in private why they were not able to cast the demon out. Jesus replied: "This
kind can come out by nothing but prayer and fasting" (Mark 9:29).

This explains the *powers* kind of fallen angel. Jesus called it "this
kind." It is powerful and militant. It will remain in a person as long as
possible and cause alarming distraction, confusion, fear, and sorrow,
even to the point of death. Its goal is to enjoy using the person's body
and ultimately, to destroy him. It may have a group of others and together they will invade a life. This was true of the demoniac at Gadara
(Mark 5:1–20), who had thousands of demons possessing him. The Lord
explained that even if they are morally expelled through reform, the demons will return with enough other demons to conquer the individual
if he is not born-again (Matthew 12:43–45).

The believer is likely to find himself in combat with this powerful
kind of fallen angel. They are stubborn, arrogant, and determined to
have their way. They refuse to obey any command but Satan's. If their
victim is also under the influence of drugs and alcohol, the problem is
compounded. The strength of the control demon is increased by the
intoxicating substance. Only through a righteous life, prevailing prayer,
and determination of faith can it be cast out, because the faith necessary
is more difficult to be created in the exorcist. The prayer and fasting are
to get us focused on spiritual things, for us to confess sins and to give
ourselves wholly to Christ as Lord of our lives. This kind of demon is
filthy, aggressive, and sometimes cheeky. They hate our Lord, the Bible,
their victims, and hearing about the cross and resurrection of Jesus. They
are spiritual bullies, but they must obey a direct command by the Spirit
of God to leave their victim alone or to leave you alone.

The Rulers of the Darkness of This Age. This Greek term has four words in it: *kosmokratoras tou skotous toutou.* It means "the world rulers of this darkness." "This darkness" is caused by evil and rebellion in all forms when Satan is in control of a person or a place. This "darkness" is an important word in the Bible. It is a representation of evil in all its forms. Underneath the darkness is Satan's hatred of the Son of God. There is no better study of the scriptural meaning of darkness than the three hours of darkness when Jesus was crucified and Satan had complete control of the world.

Parenthesis: Darkness Over All the Earth
(Matthew 27:45; Luke 23:44; Mark 15:33)

Jesus was nailed to the cross at eight or nine in the morning on Friday, April 7, AD 30, according to most reliable biblical chronologists. At noon, a blanket of darkness covered the earth and lasted for three hours.

> Now when the sixth hour had come, there was darkness over the whole land until the ninth hour. And at the ninth hour Jesus cried out with a loud voice, saying, "Eloi, Eloi, lama sabachthani?" which is translated, "My God, My God, why have You forsaken Me?" (Mark 15:33–34)

> Now it was about the sixth hour and there was darkness over all the earth until the ninth hour. Then the sun was darkened, and the veil of the temple was torn in two. And when Jesus had cried with a loud voice, He said, "Father, into Your hands I commit My spirit." Having said this, He breathed His last. (Luke 23:44–46)

At noon, the sun was at its zenith, but a mysterious darkness fell over the cross of Jesus and covered everything else, even the execution detail and townspeople who had gathered to watch the gruesome sight. It spread outward from the hill where the Romans crucified malefactors. The New Testament consistently uses the Greek word *ge,* pronounced "ghay," as the common term for "earth." The source of that darkness was not an eclipse of the sun. Jesus was crucified on Passover, and Passover comes at full moon.

The darkness was supernatural in origin. It was specifically related to the death of Jesus and the Father forsaking Him during the three hours of darkness. It was satanic, the result of the devil's power becoming dominant over the earth during that time. The sky was filled with something so dark it prevented the light of the sun from shining through.

The Father had forsaken Him. In Psalm 22, it was prophesied:

> My God, My God, why have You forsaken Me?
> Why are You so far from helping Me,
> and from the words of My groaning?
> O My God, I cry in the daytime, but you do not hear;
> and in the night season and am not silent. (Psalm 22:1–2)

The darkness descended, the Father forsook Him, and Jesus screamed in pain and in the agony of absolute loneliness. The guilt and punishment of our sins had been laid on Him.

> For He made Him who knew no sin to be sin for us, that we might become the righteousness of God in Him. (2 Corinthians 5:21)

The devil knew that the body of Jesus was in an emaciated condition resulting from the scourging and beatings and from being impaled on a cross. Death was imminent. His plan was to attack Him while He was helpless and alone, so weak He was unable to carry His cross. Satan would take Jesus's life from Him by killing Him before He was able to offer up His life to the Father as a sin offering. To make sure he killed Jesus, Satan attacked Him, using a sky filled with fallen angels, who assaulted Him in a frenzy of hatred never known to any of us. He would kill Jesus and prevent Him from laying down His life, as an act of His own will, as He had promised to do.

> My Father loves Me because I lay down My life that I may take it again. No one takes it from Me, but I lay it down of Myself. I have power to lay it down, and I have power to take it again. This command I have received from My Father. (John 10:17–18)

If Satan and his demonic hordes could take Jesus's life from Him, it would end God's plan of salvation for humankind. It would mean that the Savior would be conquered by the very sin and darkness He came to conquer for us. The adversary summoned his dark angels to crush the spirit of the God Man, with their ominous presence and power engulfing the earth. They would use their power of death on Him in such a violent torrent of wicked energy from millions of evil angels that Jesus was sure to expire. Then, at last, Satan could be "like God," and the kingdom of darkness would rule over the kingdom of light.

The darkness, then, was the result of Satan's evil power temporarily becoming dominant over Jesus. The shock effect, Satan mused, would be enough to kill Jesus. He would not be able to sustain the death blow of depravity so immense that His super-weakened condition would collapse. Maximum evil would attack maximum holiness and produce a victory for the kingdom of darkness in a show of force so great, the world would be forced to take notice. That was Satan's plan.

Lucifer's gigantic pride overloaded his estimation of Jesus Christ. He thought the combined effects of the human abuse and the suffocating onslaught of earth's atmosphere filled with dark spirits would be enough to take Jesus's life from Him. But the beatings did not take His life. Being scourged with a flagellum—a whip made from leather thongs studded with metal and bone tips—did not take it. The nails driven into His hands and feet did not kill Him. When the darkness lifted, around three o'clock that afternoon, Jesus was still alive and in control of His will, mind, and speech. The authority of His status as the Son of God returned. The inner veil of the grand temple was torn apart from top to bottom, and the way to God and heaven was opened.

The gospels record that Jesus cried out with a scream, just before He gave up His spirit to the Father. Why the loud scream? The demons had violently convulsed Him in a final, overwhelming paroxysm which would provide the final blow. It is likely that it was Jesus's scream of pain as He suffered that final attack upon His body, soul, and spirit. Even such a death blow did not kill Him, however. As an act of His own will, He handed over His spirit to the Father and then died. Satan's ultimate plan had failed. The apostle John said: "The light shines in the darkness, and the darkness did not overcome it" (John 1:5 NRSV).

We understand the nature of this darkness. It is so evil as to cover the entire world and to try to kill the sinless Son of God. These demons are responsible for distributing wickedness throughout the entire world during this age. They create centers of evil power in organizations, institutions, educational systems, religions, entertainment, politics, government, sports, the arts, transportation, communication systems, toy makers, photography, and human hearts. The list goes on and on, covering the universe. If humans ever live on the moon, the devil will infect that world with his darkness and death. The invisible war is a universal war.

Parenthesis Closed

We have reviewed three of the four groups of angels in Satan's command structure: principalities, powers, and the rulers of the darkness of this present age. The fourth satanic organization in hell's hierarchy is:

The Spiritual Hosts of Wickedness in the Heavenly Places. As we have reconnoitered our enemy, we have discovered that the first three levels of fallen angels have command roles. *Principalities* are the top commanders who oversee the evil operations of the devil all over the world. *Powers* are combat commanders, something like our division commanders who hold the ranks of generals. They are warlike and aggressive, and their duty is to train and direct the fallen angels in launching campaigns against Christianity and the values derived from the Bible such as virtue, honesty, transparency, kindness, love, and decency.

At this moment, the campaign to take over and destroy the United States of America is gaining power. Unless revival comes, we will go the way all Reformation-era nations have gone. They were created by the great Christian movements of the Reformation. Now they are secularistic, atheistic or on the verge of it, and destined for the junkyard of nations that forgot God. Will America join them?

The spiritual hosts of wickedness in the heavenly places describes the vast numbers of evil angels who are carrying out the commands of the top leaders. The words used by Paul tell us a lot.

First, they are *spiritual* beings—fallen angels—and they are not susceptible to human power or planning of any sort. Our war against them must be of a spiritual nature. They are invisible but real. They have the created abilities that God's angels have, only totally evil. They can see, hear, and travel at the speed of light, and each possesses intellect, emotions, and a will that is sold out to their leader, Satan.

Second, they are *hosts,* which means large numbers or armies of angels.

Third, they are *wicked*, through and through. Not one has a modicum of goodness.

Fourth, they live and operate in the *heavenly places.* Paul isn't speaking of the heaven of God as he writes this. There are three "heavens" mentioned in the Bible. The third heaven is the abode of God, His angels, and the spirits of all the saints who have died. The second heaven is what we call "outer space." It is where the planets are located. The demons are quartered in the space all around planet Earth. Many are in our atmosphere and are immediately near to all of us. The first heaven is where the birds fly. Many demons are located around earth and are in possession of humans and human activities. They sometimes inhabit animals (see Mark 5:9–14).

If Christians ever needed a motive for suiting up with the armor of God, this is it. Let the nearness of Satan's presence and millions of fallen angels sink in. The devil is out on the hunt, every day.

> Be sober, be vigilant; because your adversary the devil
> walks about like a roaring lion, seeking whom he may
> devour. Resist him, steadfast in the faith, knowing that
> the same sufferings are experienced by your brotherhood
> in the world. (1 Peter 5:8–9)

To "resist" him in the faith is to oppose him, to withstand his advances. We must take an offensive stand toward Satan and all his dark angels and kingdom of darkness, by using Scripture. "Steadfast in the faith" means living in consistent obedience to Jesus, walking by the Spirit of God.

Conclusion

Our spiritual combat in the invisible army makes the armor of God essential. We're facing an army of evil angels, any one of whom is capable of destroying an entire city. They are well organized and committed to the destruction of anyone and everything connected with God. The following chapter tells us how to defend against the hierarchy of hell and take the offensive against them.

Five

The Believer's Armory of Spiritual Weapons

> Put on the whole armor of God, that you may be able to stand against the wiles of the devil. (Ephesians 6:11)

> For though we walk in the flesh, we do not war according to the flesh. For the weapons of our warfare are not carnal but mighty in God for pulling down strongholds, casting down arguments and every high thing that exalts itself against the knowledge of God, bringing every thought into captivity to the obedience of Christ, and being ready to punish all disobedience when your obedience is fulfilled. (2 Corinthians 10:3–6)

Christians are up against the hosts of hell every day of their lives. They come from many directions in multiple ways. Paul identifies some of them in the passage above:

Strongholds. These are concentrations of evil power that make it impossible for any Christian to overcome them in his own strength. I often see examples of them. A person is addicted to alcohol or drugs, under control by one or more demons, and committed to a pattern of thinking that makes him imagine that he has no problem. In Paul's day, a stronghold was a city with a high wall around it or a military defense built to prevent enemy encroachments. In our day it is easy for a person to "wall" God out of his life.

Imaginations, arguments. These refer to patterns of thinking that seek to disprove God in some way. They usually argue from a false premise. It is in this way that agnostics think they are proving that the resurrection of Jesus is a myth. They argue that, since the dead cannot live again, then Christ could not have come back to life. They ignore the powerful historical evidence that shows that He was raised as reported and seen by hundreds of eyewitnesses who were willing to die in support of that truth.

High things. One of the devil's tactics is to place an atheist or agnostic in a place of great influence and use him or her to motivate people within their circle of influence to disbelieve the Scriptures and disobey God. Politicians, professors, some preachers, and even some parents can be used by Satan to turn the lives of people under them toward a worldview that corrupts the thought life of millions of young people. Institutions, positions, and organizations can also be "high things." Whatever or whoever is in a position of authority over people, and uses the authority to discredit God or prevent people from obeying Him, is a "high thing."

God's Armor Is Our Armory

Unless we are properly prepared, the demon army will destroy us. Preparation begins with taking up the weapons in our spiritual armory. Paul called it "the armor of God." He used the Greek word, *panoplia,* which means "all the weapons."

Every modern military installation has an "arms room," where all their weapons are kept under lock and key. The Christian army has several weapons. Paul showed them to us by using an analogy, the Roman soldier. Rome's thirty legions were stationed across the empire. Each of them had about six thousand combat soldiers, along with specialists such as surgeons. Attached to each legion was a cavalry unit of more than a hundred mounted lancers.

We will name each weapon of the Roman armory mentioned by Paul, and then give the spiritual meaning of each.

For the Emotions: The belt of truth. The leather belt girded the waist and had several uses. It held a tunic of thick material in place. The bottom edges were tucked under the belt to give freedom of movement when running, marching, or fighting. It was wide enough to reach from the waist down to the thighs. Hanging on the left side was the soldier's dagger. On the right side hung his sword, and on the front hung a studded leather apron which protected his private area.

The Scripture says, "Stand, therefore, having girded your waist with truth" (Ephesians 6:14). There are two sides to truth. There is objective truth, which is the Bible, the Word of God. In His prayer in John 17, our Lord said to the Father, "Your Word is truth" (vs. 17). When we read the Scriptures, we are reading objective truth which the Holy Spirit inspired the human authors to write down. It is eternal and alive with the way of everlasting life. It never changes and cannot be annulled or broken (John 10:35). We are warned not to tamper with it nor try to add anything to it (Revelation 22:18–19).

Subjectively, the Word can be lodged inside our minds through our memory. It is the settled conviction within us that God's Word is altogether true and worthy of our faithfulness to believe and obey it. King David wrote, "Your word I have hidden in my heart, that I might not sin against You" (Psalm 119:11).

Satan is sure to attack us in this vital area. The belt protected the loins of the soldier who wore it. This calls our attention to our emotions, especially our sexuality. Nothing cripples our faith as easily as sexual sin and the emotional baggage it carries with it, such as guilt, anger, hatred, confusion, revenge, and more. When the enemy strikes us a blow in this area it can ruin us, our family relationships, our testimony, and much more. In this day of blatant permissiveness and sexual images everywhere we turn, our strongest defense is the influence of the Word of God on our moral lives. It will have little influence on us unless we commit it to our minds and spirits by reading it daily. We need both objective and subjective truth.

More than anything, Satan wants to take away the influence of the Bible on our thinking. He will discredit the Bible, attempting to convince us that it is made up of old stories from days long ago and has no bearing on life today. He will fill our minds with TV, movies, books, magazines, and the wicked lives of public figures to keep us from reading it. He will try to convince us that science has disproven the Bible, including its central message of Jesus Christ as the Son of God, who came to earth, took our humanity, accepted the penalty for our sins by dying on the cross, was buried, and rose again on the third day.

When I became a Christian, I was eleven years of age, but I realized that a big change had taken place in my life. I wanted a Bible, so I saved my allowance of twenty-five cents a week to order one out of the Montgomery Ward catalog. Before I was saved, I used my allowance to buy BB's for my BB gun. After I received Jesus into my heart, I used it to buy my first Bible.

For the Spiritual Vitals: The breastplate of righteousness. The Roman soldier's breastplate (called the *thorax*) protected that part of his body from the neck down his chest and back and was fitted about two inches below the top of the belt. Paul likens the breastplate to righteousness, which is being right and doing right, with Christ Himself as the absolute standard. God gives us the righteousness of Christ through the indwelling presence and power of the Holy Spirit. The Spirit works righteousness in our thinking, feeling, and doing, as we yield our lives completely to Him. Works of righteousness are produced through Him and not through our prideful flesh.

The Roman soldier's vital organs—his heart and lungs, with other smaller organs—were covered front and back by the breastplate. The inward nature and outward power of the righteous life of Jesus act as the quality of the born-again life as well as the vitality of that life, which is nothing less than the risen life of Jesus:

> I have been crucified with Christ; it is no longer I who
> live, but Christ lives in me; and the life which I now live
> in the flesh I live by faith in the Son of God, who loved
> me and gave Himself for me. (Galatians 2:20)

Where, in us, does Christ live? In the heart. Not the physical organ but the spiritual center, the control room. The Bible calls it the "heart" because it is the "cockpit," so to speak, the center, the heart of the life. The righteousness of Christ keeps and controls the life of a true believer in Jesus Christ.

The enemy's chief weapon against the righteousness of Christ is works-righteousness. How often have I heard people protest an invitation to become a Christian by saying, "I'm as good as people in your church!" Outwardly, this is often true, but God will not accept self-righteousness. The apostle Paul, who lived an exemplary life religiously, admitted that God would not accept a legalistic kind of righteousness:

> Brethren, my heart's desire and prayer to God for Israel
> is that they may be saved. For I bear them witness that
> they have a zeal for God, but not according to knowl-
> edge. For they being ignorant of God's righteousness,
> and seeking to establish their own righteousness, have
> not submitted to the righteousness of God. (Romans
> 10:1–3)

Legalistic righteousness, or works-righteousness, is man attempting to make himself good by keeping religious laws, ordinances, and traditions. Works-righteousness is produced by human pride. If it could please God, Christ would not have come to earth and died for our sins. God will only accept the goodness which is through faith in His Son. Again, Paul says something we need to hear:

> Yet indeed I also count all things loss for the excellence
> of the knowledge of Christ Jesus my Lord, for whom
> I have suffered the loss of all things, and count them

as rubbish, that I may gain Christ and be found in Him, not having my own righteousness, which is from the law, but that which is through faith in Christ, the righteousness which is from God by faith. (Philippians 3:8–9)

By depending on self-righteousness, we give ourselves credit for a righteous life we think we have, and we rob God by refusing to accept the righteousness of faith which He alone provides in Jesus.

For the Footing: The boots of confidence in the gospel. The soldier's boots were an essential weapon in the armory. They were crafted with thick leather. The soles were fitted with hobnails, which acted like the cleats on today's football or baseball shoes. A Roman soldier could not afford to be knocked off his feet. Paul uses the word *stand* four times in this passage, and said "and having done all, to stand." He meant to say something like, "Whatever you do, stay on your feet!" To keep his feet sturdy, he wore hobnail boots.

The New King James Version of Ephesians 6:15 reads, "And having shod your feet with the preparation of the gospel of peace." A modern translation of the Greek word that is translated "preparation" is "firm footing," according to the New Greek-English Interlinear New Testament. The NRSV has it, "whatever will make you ready." It seems that, with the emphasis on "standing" in the context, the wisest choice is "firm footing."

We know from the information given us by history and archaeology that most of the combat soldiers wore boots or sandals with hobnails for the very reason that they needed firm footing in close combat warfare. This part of our armor illustrates the soldier's need for assurance that his feet would not slip. He was not prepared to go out to battle unless he was confident that, when the fight was over, he would still be standing.

We are not prepared to live the life of a Christian, which includes witnessing our faith, teaching our children, and defending our faith, unless we are confident that the gospel is true:

Moreover, brethren, I declare to you the gospel which I preached to you, which also you received and in which you stand, by which also you are saved, if you hold fast that word which I preached to you—unless you believed in vain.

For I delivered to you first of all that which I also received: that Christ died for our sins according to the Scriptures, and that He was buried, and that He rose again the third day according to the Scriptures, and that He was seen by Cephas, then by the twelve After that He was seen by over five hundred brethren at once, of whom the greater part remain to the present, but some have fallen asleep. After that He was seen by James, then by all the apostles. Then last of all He was seen by me also, as by one born out of due time. (1 Corinthians 15:1–8)

The common argument against the resurrection of Jesus is that it is scientifically impossible for the dead to rise. The biblical argument in support of the fact of Jesus' resurrection is historical. Not "could He have risen" but "*did* He rise again?" In the passage above, Paul lists the more prominent people who saw Him alive following His crucifixion. More than five hundred at one time saw and heard Him. The apostles all witnessed His resurrection. They saw Him, touched Him, heard Him, ate with Him, and were willing to die for the historical truth of that event.

Being prepared to carry the good news of the gospel made it necessary for the apostles to have confidence in what they preached, just as a soldier needed confidence in his ability to stay on his feet during a battle. No one would die for a known lie. All those men died for their faith as martyrs except John, who suffered torture and imprisonment on the island of Patmos. Paul, who wrote the passage above, was in prison when he wrote the letter to the Ephesians and was condemned to die. He could have saved his life by denying that Jesus had risen and embracing the gods of Rome. He could not deny a truth that was being vindicated by the deaths of thousands of Christians. They, too, accepted martyrdom instead of saving their own lives.

Paul was eventually beheaded on orders of Nero, emperor of Rome. He was taken to the outskirts of Rome on the Ostian Way. As he knelt in prayer, a soldier executed him.

Protection against Temptation: The shield of the faith. Each Roman combat soldier carried a shield in his left hand because he used his right hand for his weapon of attack. This shield was called a "door shield" because it was large enough for him to crouch behind. It was about four feet long and two and a half feet wide. Several soldiers could stand their door shields next to each other, making a "fence" for them to kneel behind as a group. The unit's colors were painted on the front of the shield. Handles were fastened to the opposite side, making it easy for the soldier to hold it with his left hand and use his weapon with the right.

In Paul's analogy, the shield illustrates faith. Some translations say, *"the shield of faith."* However, the original language of the Greek New Testament reads, *"the shield of the faith."* The definite article, *the*, implies that Paul is referring to faith as the objective body of truth, the Scriptures. Both objective and subjective faith are attacked by Satan. Objectively, our faith rests on the body of truth, the Bible. Subjectively, we believe that it is true and that it is true for anyone.

If the devil and his dark angels can destroy our assurance that the Scriptures are true, then we will lose our personal trust in anything it says that is related to eternal life, and we will lose our defenses against the lies they tell us. "The fiery darts of the wicked one" (Ephesians 6:16) are the lies and temptations that Satan camouflages to look like truth. We notice that Paul said:

> Above all, taking the shield of faith with which you will
> be able to quench all the fiery darts of the wicked one.
> (Ephesians 6:16)

He does not mean that the shield is the most important piece of armor, but that it covers everything else, the soldier and all his equipment, to protect him from Satan's "fire arrows."

Soldiers in ancient times, including the Romans, learned that an enemy shield could be compromised by being set on fire with arrows dipped in asphalt. At various places in Asia and Europe there could be found pits of tar, called bitumen. That substance was highly flammable, just like it is now. Arrow tips dipped in it and ignited were shot into an enemy's shield, and it would catch the shield's covering on fire. Shields were made of two wooden planks glued together in a convex shape, then covered with canvas, then calfskin. These would easily burn. When the enemy soldier discarded his flaming shield, he could easily be subdued. The Romans began adding sheets of metal to the covering, which the arrows could not penetrate. It is this later model that Paul has in mind.

Satan's lies are like fire arrows. They will destroy our defenses unless we take up the shield of faith. He will penetrate our thoughts with fleshly desires, as he did to Eve. Like the fire arrow, they compromise weak defenses. The shield of the faith, whether we mean objective or subjective faith, will stop the lies from penetrating our thought life and influencing us to sin against God. When the devil tempted Jesus, He responded each time with the Scripture, saying, *"It is written!"* That was objective faith. When King David wrote Psalm 119:11, he spoke of subjective faith: "Your word I have hidden in my heart, that I might not sin against You."

For the Thought Life: The helmet of salvation. In the dust and blood of battle, the soldier's head will become a target for his enemy. Our brain, eyes, ears, nose, and mouth are all in the head. A sharp blow from a sword or dagger or a crushing blow from a battle-ax would likely mean death. It appears that the apostle has the Christian's thought life mostly in mind, although the other organs affect the way our brain operates.

The Roman helmet was made of metal or thick leather that the blow of a sword could not penetrate. On the rear of the helmet was a neck guard. Hinged cheekpieces protected the ears and sides of the face.

One of the devil's often-used arrows is doubt that we are truly saved. Causing us to doubt our salvation makes us tentative, fearful, and weak in our faith. Our courage is lost, and our joy vanishes. I have frequently heard believers, especially young ones, pour out their fears about locking horns with temptation because they doubted that they would go to heaven if they died. I have heard older members of churches say that they have been "saved" several times, because they can't stop wanting to commit a certain sin or because they have asked God to give them assurance but still "feel lost."

Keeping our thoughts straight about being saved is a matter of maintaining a regular time of fellowship with the Lord every day, which includes Bible reading and prayer. When I was a young Christian and doubt, temptation, or fear pushed at me, I learned that remembering the wonderful experience of my salvation would reassure me. It was that way with King David, apparently, when he wrote,

> O God the Lord, the strength of my salvation,
> You have covered my head in the day of battle. (Psalm
> 140:7)

To him, the assurance of his salvation was like a helmet covering his head in battle.

Our Primary Weapon: The sword of the Spirit. The Roman soldier's sword was his primary weapon, like an infantryman's rifle today. It was about two feet long, hanging off his right hip in a scabbard. It was two-edged, with the point and edges sharpened. Scripture uses the sword as an analogy for the Bible, the Word of God:

> The Word of God is living and powerful, and sharper
> than any two-edged sword, piercing even to the divi-
> sion of soul and spirit, and of joints and marrow, and
> is a discerner of the thoughts and intents of the heart.
> (Hebrews 4:12)

This verse describes the spiritual power of the Scriptures. The Holy Spirit inspired it, just as the Apostle Peter has said, "holy men of God spoke as they were moved by the Holy Spirit" (2 Peter 1:21). He not only inspired it, but He has overseen the transmission of the Bible over centuries and into many languages.

Since the Holy Spirit inspired the Scriptures, the regenerated spirit of the child of God can receive it. The Word is alive, the born-again spirit is alive, so the very life of God flows from His Word to His children. It carries His power and authority. It conquers Satan and every evil thing he throws at us.

Satan hates the Bible because it is our most powerful weapon against him. It will uncover his lies, his false love, his schemes, and his empty happiness. When it is applied honestly to an issue, it opens and exposes all aspects of it. The devil's lies are shown for their insidious nature. It is like a physician doing a post-mortem: all parts and their relationships are brought to light and explained. The cancerous growth of evil is magnified and can be removed. It is "alive" and "powerful".

Sharper means "able to cut with a single stroke."

Piercing means "penetrating," able to separate soul from spirit so as to understand them both. The same is true of joints and marrow in bones.

The Bible is the tool of discernment, which is the ability to judge a word or nuance in the light of God's truth, against which any word, act, or thought can be compared. If it does not agree with the Word, it has missed the mark.

Praying and Watching. Paul continues by telling us how to build up the person inside the armor. The finest weapons do little good if the soldier is weak and fearful. Notice that we are placed on guard duty during this age of evil:

> Praying always with all prayer and supplication in the Spirit, watching to this end with all perseverance and supplication for all saints—and for me, that utterance may be given to me, that I may open my mouth boldly to make known the mystery of the gospel, for which I am an ambassador in chains; that in it I may speak boldly, as I ought to speak. (Ephesians 6:18–20)

As we put on our armor, we must accept it "praying" and "watching."

Praying. When Paul wrote this letter to the Ephesian church, he was a prisoner in Rome's Mamertine Prison. He was chained to a wall or a heavy weight. He had been consigned to the filthy lower dungeon called "the Tullianum" in almost total darkness. When he was brought out and given opportunity to speak, he proclaimed Christ crucified, risen, and coming again. His only fear was that his frail body would shrink back from any more punishment and be quiet. There were people around him, soldiers, jailers, and other prisoners. When he had opportunity to give his defense before Caesar Nero, he wanted to open his mouth boldly and witness the gospel. He asked the church of Ephesus, and others who would hear this letter read, to pray for him. He did not ask for deliverance from prison but for utterance when he saw an opening to witness the faith to all who would hear.

His request was built around two participles: *praying* and *watching.* Both are intensified by the word *all,* which means "all kinds of prayer." *Supplication* means "petitioning God out of a deep need." Paul had some basic needs, such as comfort, better food, or clothing to ward off the dark and cold of the dungeon. His greatest need was for the courage and strength to speak the gospel of Jesus Christ.

Watching calls to mind the watchmen on the walls of ancient cities, including Jerusalem. If they saw an enemy coming, they were to warn the people with the blast of a trumpet. It was their duty to be ready for the battle.

> "But if the watchman sees the sword coming and does not blow the trumpet, and the people are not warned, and the sword comes and takes any person from among them, he is taken away in his iniquity; but his blood I will require at the watchman's hand."

> So you, son of man: I have made you a watchman for the house of Israel; therefore you shall hear a word from My mouth and warn them for Me. (Ezekiel 33:6–7)

The enemy takes many forms, on mission fields, in our homes and neighborhoods, in our political process, educational systems, and entertainment and news media, and against our churches. Of special importance are our children.

God will supply the needed courage and conviction, just as He did for the early apostles and preachers who faced the dark angels in their day. We are struggling against those same enemies. The demons who plotted the arrest, persecution, and execution of Paul and the other apostles are plotting against us. We are in the same spiritual combat with them in the invisible war. Paul's analogy, using the Roman soldier's armor, illustrates our spiritual weapons as we face spiritual combat.

Conclusion: The Armor of God

The armor of God means all the weapons God has given us for the invisible war. We cannot fight a spiritual battle and win without all the weapons.

- The *belt of truth* protects our emotional life and provides for the Sword of the Spirit.
- The *breastplate of righteousness* protects the spiritual life, which is centered in the regenerated spirit, called "the heart." It is occupied by the Holy Spirit, who lives out the risen life of Jesus and makes it possible for the believer to live a righteous life.
- The *boots of confidence in the gospel* give believers the firm footing they need when doing battle with Satan's angels.
- The *shield of faith* quenches the flaming arrows of temptation and satanic deception.
- The *helmet of salvation* guards against the lies of Satan in our thought life by keeping us focused on the reality of our salvation.
- The *sword of the Spirit* is the Word of God, the Bible, which is the believer's primary weapon. The truth and power of the Spirit of God flow from its pages and give us victory over every attack of the devil. There is no true Christianity apart from the Bible.
- *Praying and watching* help keep the person inside the armor strong and courageous, able always to withstand in the evil day, and having done all, to remain standing after combat.

Six

YOUR SPIRITUAL LIFE: HOW TO BE STRONG IN THE LORD

Years ago, a jetliner took off from a midwestern airport with 107 passengers and crew. In the climb-out, two of its three engines suddenly shut down, and it began losing power. The captain radioed "mayday" to the tower, and the crew quickly began looking for the problem by going back through their checklist. They discovered a fuel switch still in the "off" position. The two engines had been starved of fuel. When they flipped it to "on," the idle engines surged with power. Someone had failed to turn on a crucial control switch, but the checklist had saved them all.

The Bible is the Christian's checklist. Perhaps someone who is reading this has lost power in his or her spiritual life. I will take you through its power check, and you will see how to "be strong in the Lord and in the power of His might" (Ephesians 6:10). This checklist shows every step in the process of living by means of the Holy Spirit.

Consciousness: Be Conscious of Your Sins

I acknowledge my transgressions,
and my sin is always before me.
Against You, You only, have I sinned,
and done this evil in Your sight. (Psalm 51:3–4)

King David wrote Psalm 51 as a way of confessing his sins of adultery and murder. He had been burdened with guilt from the time they happened. Most sins are not as dramatic as David's, and we tend to let the remembrance of them float off into the past and get lost. Unconfessed sin causes our fellowship with God to be broken. When we lose it, we lose our power, just like the jetliner. When that happens, we must get busy looking for the cause. It will almost always be sin that we have not acknowledged to God. It may have happened a long time ago, and we have forgotten all about it, but the Lord has not forgotten!

Jesus died for our sins, and when we accept Him as Savior and Lord, the guilt is removed, and we are made His children forever. The relationship is secure. When a Christian sins, however, fellowship with Christ through the Spirit is broken. Spiritual power shuts down. We may even feel that we were never saved. Our joy and freedom go away, and we begin feeling guilty and alienated from the Lord. We need to confess all sins to Him and ask Him to cleanse our conscience, the way David did in Psalm 51.

Confession: Confess Any and All Sins

The blood of Jesus covers the believer's sins, but the Lord demands that His people acknowledge their sins through a prayer of confession. As the Holy Spirit brings your sins to mind, confess them, and do not stop until the slate is clean. A dear friend of mine, now in heaven, used to say, "Keep short accounts with God." Once you have confessed a sin, then forsake it, and ask God to give you the power to say no to temptation.

Notice what the apostle John says about guilt and confession:

If we say that we have fellowship with Him and walk in darkness, we lie and do not practice the truth. But if we walk in the light as He is in the light, we have fellowship with one another, and the blood of Jesus Christ His Son cleanses us from all sin.

If we say that we have no sin, we deceive ourselves and the truth is not in us. If we confess our sins, He is faithful and just to forgive us our sins and to cleanse us from all unrighteousness. If we say that we have not sinned, we make Him a liar, and His word is not in us. (1 John 1:6–10)

Cleansing:
Expect Confessed Sins to be Forgiven and
Cleansed from Your Conscience

Once a sincere confession is made, you will sense a freedom in your heart from feelings of guilt as the Spirit frees up your conscience. Joy, power, peace, comfort, and assurance return. A word of caution is necessary, however. You will not sense the freedom unless all known sins are confessed. If you hold back and refuse to deal with one or more sins, the Holy Spirit will continue to be grieved, and the guilt feelings will stay with you. If this happens, you know that part of your sin account has not been dealt with honestly. It may also be that you have not dealt with another person who has been hurt by your sin and made confession to them.

Commitment: Commit Your Cleansed Personality to the Lord

Often, when the life has been cleansed, you may sense that God had something for you to do for Him that was interrupted by sin episodes. Once you sense His forgiveness, His call upon your life will be renewed. Be willing to do it, as Isaiah was. Once he became conscious of a particular sin, he confessed it and was cleansed. Then he heard the call of God:

> Also, I heard the voice of the Lord saying,
>> "Whom shall I send,
>> and who will go for us?"
> Then I said, "Here am I! Send me!" (Isaiah 6:8)

Consecration: The Holy Spirit Will Then Consecrate You to His Service

To consecrate is to set apart someone or something for God's special purpose. One of the clearest acts of consecration in the Bible is that of Jeremiah:

> Then the LORD put forth His hand and touched my mouth, and the LORD said to me:
>> "Behold, I have put My words in your mouth.
>> See, I have this day set you over the nations and over the kingdoms,
>> to root down and to pull down,
>> to destroy and to throw down,
>> to build and to plant." (Jeremiah 1:9–10)

Control: Once We Are Consecrated, the Holy Spirit Controls Us

The Spirit's control of the life of a believer is called "the filling." Since He lives in our born-again spiritual nature, He operates from there. He controls the mind, and the mind controls the body. In this way, He uses us by empowering our spiritual gifts, which are the spiritual abilities given for ministry in the body of Christ. There are about twenty of them. Each believer has at least one, but usually, one is primary, and the others cluster around it to form a complete ministry. Also, the Spirit empowers each function of our armor because the devil will become aggressive toward us, to destroy the effectiveness of our filling.

Communication: The Believer, Under the Spirit's Control, Then Communicates Christ, In Us, To Us, and Through Us

Then, the checklist finished, the genuine Christian life is lived out, as Paul expressed it to the Galatian church:

> I have been crucified with Christ; it is no longer I who live but Christ Who lives in me; and the life which I now live in the flesh I live by faith in the Son of God, who loved me and gave Himself for me. (Galatians 2:20)

The Power Checklist

As you go down the list, go back a page or two and read the explanation:

1. *Consciousness* of sin.
2. *Confession* of each and every sin.
3. *Cleansing* of the conscience.
4. *Commitment* of the cleansed life to Christ. Also called "surrender."
5. *Consecration* of the cleansed life by the Holy Spirit.
6. *Control*, also called "filling of the Spirit."
7. *Communication* Christ living in the believer.

Seven

VICTORY IN JESUS

Therefore He says:

> "When He ascended on high,
> He led captivity captive
> and gave gifts to men." (Ephesians 4:8)

Our study of angels began with their creation by the Son of God at a time before He came into the world. The highest and greatest of the archangels that He created, who was Lucifer, led a revolt against Him, joined by a third of the other angels. When Jesus came to earth, He recalled seeing the defeat of Lucifer in the first battle between Jesus and Satan.

> And He said to them, "I beheld Satan as lightning fall
> from heaven." (Luke 10:18)

Later, with Jesus on earth in human flesh, Satan saw opportunities to defeat Him. He tried to tempt Him to sin, as he did Adam and Eve and the rest of humanity. Each temptation failed as Jesus employed the Word of God against him (Matthew 4:1–11).

The Crucifixion and Resurrection

Satan planned to make Jesus's crucifixion his moment of victory. He took possession of Judas Iscariot, who betrayed the Son of God with a kiss. He orchestrated six illegal trials and trumped-up charges to get Him crucified. Already beaten and bloody, the Son of God was nailed to a cross and suspended between God and man.

Satan waited until Jesus was forsaken by God the Father for three hours, alone, helpless, and at the point of death. He then unleashed all his dark angels to attack Him for those three hours. Satan was in complete control of the world as Jesus was dealt one near-lethal blow after another in His spirit, soul, and body, and the Father turned away from Him. From noontime until three o'clock the sun was darkened by the presence of many fallen, wicked angels. Expecting Him to be dead as the darkness lifted, Satan must have been shocked to see Him still alive and in control of His faculties, as the darkness lifted. Satan heard Him give up His life to the Father as the offering for our sins. Lucifer lost again.

The lifeless body of Jesus was laid in a rock tomb on Friday of Passover week. The giant stone at the entrance was sealed with Caesar's insignia. Two of God's angels were sent to break the official seal and open it early on Sunday morning. They weren't sent to let Jesus out but to let eyewitnesses inside the tomb. Peter and John were the first to look inside. They found it empty.

Beginning with the creation of the universe and mankind, Satan made plans to destroy everything and everyone God had created. He began with our first parents: Adam and Eve. Through clever lies and deception, he seduced them into rebelling against God by lusting for self-godhood. He continues these lies today, promising that we can be our own gods and determine for ourselves what is right and wrong.

To all of us who refuse to be duped by the devil, Jesus has promised eternal life with Him if we will but accept Him as our Savior and Lord. Philip was sent to an Ethiopian who asked to be baptized.

Philip said, "If you believe with all your heart, you may." And he answered and said, "I believe that Jesus Christ is the Son of God." (Acts 8:37)

The Ascension

After His resurrection, Jesus showed Himself alive to hundreds of people in His immortal human body for forty days. Then He ascended into heaven, promising to return. He also has provided eternal homes for all believers (John 14:1–3).

As Jesus ascended, He passed through earth's atmosphere, then through the stratosphere, which are the first and second heavens. He passed through large numbers of angels, both good and evil, on His way into the third heaven. He passed through the evil angels, who had attacked Him during the three hours of darkness. As He processed through their dark presence, they all bowed before the Son of God, who had defeated them. All they could do was to fold their wings and confess that "Jesus is Lord!"

Two statements from Scripture tell us what happened as the Son of God ascended through the mass of good and evil angels:

> Therefore He says:
> "When He ascended on high,
> He led captivity captive
> and gave gifts to men." (Ephesians 4:8)
> Having disarmed principalities and powers, He made
> a public spectacle of them, triumphing over them in it.
> (Colossians 2:15)

Though these statements are short, they are filled with the highest drama. The ascended, glorified Lord asserted His victorious power over Satan and all demons in two ways:

He led captivity captive. Who is "captivity"? It is the fallen archangel, Lucifer, who became Satan. In Isaiah 14:17, he is called the one "who did not open the house of his prisoners." That means that it was Satan who made captives of nations of men and women and kept them in bondage forever. He was "captivity," and our ascended Lord Jesus *made him His captive!* As Jesus passed through the ranks of the evil angels, He caused them all to bow before Him as His captives, and the first one of them was the devil! Jesus humiliated Satan in front of all the angels, good and evil!

He made a public spectacle of principalities and powers. All evil angels, with Satan in front, were paraded before the angels of God. All angels who defected and joined Lucifer's rebellion are now humiliated before God and all the angels of God, as well as all the saints of God who are in heaven.

The humiliation included "disarming" the evil angels. The Greek word *apekduomai* means to "completely strip away" something from oneself. These evil angels had flung themselves on Him, at Satan's command, during the three hours of darkness. They were trying to make merciless death conquer Him, creating pain on Him that none of us can even imagine. But He just would not die! His authority over death was greater than hell's power could create.

Another dramatic word is *triumphing.* The Greek word is *thriambeuo.* It means "to celebrate a victory." It was used in hymns sung in festal celebrations.

How did the risen Lord celebrate His victory over sin and Satan? In ancient times, when a general won a great victory over his enemies, he took many prisoners and tied their hands behind them. They were led in a procession into the general's capital city as trophies of war. Jesus led captivity captive. All evil angels were defeated foes, including Satan. They were forced as spectacles before heaven and the angels of God. After judgment day comes, they will be thrown into the lake of fire forever.

Until time ends and eternity is before us, every true believer is a conqueror through Him who loved us. Until then, we join King David as he sings the Song of the King's ascension:

Lift up your heads, O you gates!
And be lifted up, you everlasting doors!
And the King of Glory shall come in.

Who is this King of Glory?
The LORD strong and mighty.
The LORD mighty in battle.
Lift up your heads, O you gates!
Lift up, you everlasting doors!
And the King of Glory shall come in.
Who is this King of Glory?
The LORD of hosts.
He is the King of glory. (Psalm 24:7–10)

Project ID: 798194
Book Title: Spiritual Combat in the Invisible War

Author: William. L. Probasco

CONCLUSION

Life without Fear

Our society seems filled with people who live in chronic fear. It drives them toward unhappy lives and, to compensate, unhealthy food, drugs, alcohol, and unlawful conduct (all of which are poor options).

Scripture warns that it is the fear of death that subjects us to bondage, and that includes those forms I just mentioned. Such fear is buried deep within our psyche. It originated with Lucifer's rebellion and man's fall into disobedience of our Creator. If you happen to be living in fear from any source, God has given us some very good news. It is about the eternal Son of God, Jesus Christ, who came to earth, died on a cross, and was raised from the dead to deliver us from death and the fear of death.

> Inasmuch then as the children have partaken of flesh and blood, He Himself likewise shared in the same, that through death He might destroy him who had the power of death, that is, the devil, and release those who through fear of death were all their lifetime subject to bondage. (Hebrews 2:14–15)

Jesus Christ can set you free from your fears by removing whatever is causing them. He then will give you the hope of eternal life. As I said in chapter 7, He permanently destroyed death's power and paraded all the disgraced dark angels before all of heaven when He returned to the Father.

He is waiting for you to ask Him to save you and set you free from any bondage. Get alone with God, and pray a prayer like this one:

> Dear Lord, I have come to You to admit that I am a sinner, and my sinful life is causing me and my loved ones a lot of grief and worry. I want to be free from my bondage of _____. I believe You are the Son of God, and You died and rose again to give me everlasting life and peace in my heart. I now surrender my life to You and accept You as My Savior and Lord. I ask You to forgive my sins and come into my life and live forever. In Jesus's name, amen.

Go to the nearest church where the Bible is taught and where they worship Jesus as the Lord. Tell them about your decision to follow Jesus. If you need help in locating such a church, let me know, and I will help you to find one.

Then please drop me a note to the address below, and tell me about your decision. Thank you for reading my book.

Dr. William L. Probasco
Church Ministry Resources
514 Valley Drive
Attalla, AL 35954

Printed in the United States
by Baker & Taylor Publisher Services